A Decade of Turmoil and Hope

A Decade of Turmoil and Hope

An Expat's Writings on Lebanon and the Arab World
(2000 - 2012)

Wissam S. Yafi

MORISKEN
VERLAG MUENCHEN

First published in 2013 by Morisken Verlag, Munich (Germany)
www.morisken-verlag.de

Cover and typesetting: Peter Sommersgutter

Library of Congress Cataloging-in-Publication Data

Yafi, Wissam S., 1970—
A Decade of Turmoil and Hope:
An Expat's Writings on Lebanon and the Arab World (2000-2012)
ISBN: 978-3-944596-02-0
1. Lebanon—Politics, government, and Cedar Revolution; 2. Arab World—Revolution and Arab Spring; 3. Democracy—Lebanon, Arab countries; 4. Iraq War; 5. The Expat Role in Lebanon and the Arab World

First edition: July 2013
Printed in the United States of America and the Federal Republic of Germany.

To Atto Zaynab & Ammo Rabi

Whose generous dinner table conversation
Has indeed been a constant source of inspiration

TABLE OF CONTENTS

INTRODUCTION
AN EXPAT'S VIEW
(2012)

INTRODUCTION: AN EXPAT'S VIEW (2012)

As I reread some of my writings over the past decade, I am almost instantly transported to the time and place in which they were written. Covering different geopolitical and socio-economic topics in Lebanon and the Arab region, I now find some are anecdotal, others journalistic, and others still editorial. I suppose the differences in style and content are a reflection of an inevitably changing mindset due to the rich variety of influencing events emanating from a highly volatile region.

In covering my native Lebanon, for instance, it is interesting to relive how the nation, in a mere decade, managed to celebrate the victory of liberating its south from Israeli occupation, then faced the misery of serial political assassinations, the triumph of its Cedar Revolution expelling Syrian forces, the pain of another war with Israel, and civil strife through a militant revolt. Throughout this period, the nation seemed destined to incessant governmental gridlock. And yet, the Lebanese people, with a relentless penchant for the good life, still managed to turn their capital, Beirut, into one of the top tourist destinations in the world!

This dichotomy takes on new dimensions if one looks at the Arab region as a whole. After a miserable decade of instability, violence, and war; and in the face of monumental challenges such as the September 11th attacks, the Iraqi invasion, a second Palestinian Intifada, Somali chaos, and Sudanese cessation; somehow the region still managed to see the miraculous conception of an Arab Spring giving hope to hundreds of millions of Arabs.

Some ask me what my principal source of writing inspiration has been. Without wanting to sound presumptuous, I find this the easiest part and readily admit that the events themselves are inspiring enough for anyone with any appetite left over to write about them. Indeed, I would as quickly concede that a Swedish expat, writing about their tranquil homeland, would have had a much harder task commenting on political and socio-economic topics back in their homeland. With the constant barrage of shell-shocking news, Lebanon and the Arab world make for quite a lot of fodder for a hungry pen.

Others point to the fact that living so far away from the region gives me the luxurious benefit of writing without any associated cost of living through it. They ask how, as an expat, I could understand what people are going through back in the region. It is a fair question and I readily admit may be true to a certain degree. Fortunately, my generation of Arab expats is also the first afforded such a highly globalized and interconnected lifestyle, which provides us constant access to news via the Internet and Satellite TV. Some I talk to in the region are surprised by how much we may be informed of what is going on halfway around the earth. They naturally assume that geography is still related to connectivity, when in reality in today's world, it isn't anymore. We see the same shows and read the same articles that they read on the very same day. Today's world also offers my generation numerous travels back to the region at a fraction of the cost. A few decades ago, this would have been limited to only those with massive resources. Living abroad has not impeded me from travelling extensively and interacting with fellow Arabs all the way from the Mashreq to the Maghreb. Of course, my interaction with the region began long before. I lived most of my youth through Lebanon's civil war, witnessed the Israeli invasion of Lebanon first hand, and survived the siege of Beirut. I saw firsthand the Arab world's development from mere desert to cosmopolitan cities.

Yes, I do live abroad; but if anything, it all makes a living example of the self-imposed exile so many of my fellow Arab expats had to go through to get a decent education and normal life. Many of us did not leave as a matter of choice any more than we could return of our own free will. Perhaps it is this yearning to one day be able to return back to our homeland, which continues to be the primary source for wanting to learn more and write about it—a meager compensation for the daily loss of cultural consumption so many of my regional compatriots take for granted. And so when some enquire about my objective in writing and whether there is some ulterior motive

INTRODUCTION

or agenda, I answer them that conversing and later writing about Lebanon and the Arab region is perhaps my own Quixotic attempt of making sense of it all, and sharing my findings with others in the hope that somehow, sometime, somewhere it will make a difference—as small as it may be. Be it with colleagues in the United States, regional experts and pundits, NGO leaders in Egypt and Morocco, economists in Syria, students in Saudi Arabia, businessmen in the UAE, taxi drivers in Bahrain or Beirut (the latter are an interesting species and a particular match to any political pundit), I find that conversing gives me insight into the different viewpoints. Analyzing and writing about it all is conceivably my feeble attempt to widen the circle of conversation, at the heart of which is a somewhat insatiable desire to reach a more measured truth on issues that affect the region and its people—one not influenced by any local allegiance, biased towards any regional ideology, or marketing any Orientalist western agenda. Rather, I would like to think that it is one, which attempts to balance a deep understanding of local and regional nuance with an appreciation of all that we have learned living in more politically and economically advanced societies.

For far too long, it saddened me that a vicious cycle hovered over a region at times seemingly as ideologically arid as its vast deserts. I have tried to remain as objective and truthful as possible throughout, uninfluenced by any specific agenda, ideology, religion, or party; but rather by what I see, read, and analyze. For instance, I was genuinely touched by my visit to the south of Lebanon and am not ashamed to admit that I wholeheartedly support the struggle of its people against Israel's injustice. I was equally swayed by the assassinations that targeted Lebanon's leaders and its democracy, and walked hand-in-hand with fellow countrymen opposed to this injustice during the Cedar Revolution. On a more regional level, I was buoyed by the United States' ousting of Iraq's dictator. And I was elatedly inspired by Arab youth in Egypt and Tunisia for their bravery and patriotism having seen and met so many of them on my trips to Cairo over the years.

Ultimately, if there has been a single-most motivation to my writings all these years, it has been to offer positive and encouraging commentary embracing positive change to a people and place I deeply care for.

WISSAM S. YAFI (August 2012)

15

SECTION ONE:
TOUR OF
LIBERATION
(2000)

Section One:
Tour Of Liberation
(2000)

The summer of 2000 would prove to be quite an eventful one. I had spent the previous winter and spring preparing every logistical nook and cranny for a research trip to Lebanon. At the time I had been living in Cambridge, Massachusetts working on my graduate studies in International Development at Harvard's Kennedy School of Government. It was a rigorous program—one of whose key requirements was a field practicum. I lobbied for a project in Lebanon justifying it as an important global crossroad, whose post-civil war development was worth studying closely. The idea was to delve into its political, economic, social and technological developments and to try and figure out its post-independence experience—both positive and negative facets. To my pleasant surprise, I received strong encouragement from the university as well as interest from several colleagues who asked if they could join me in the endeavor. It was my good fortune that two of the most qualified candidates eventually did: Theodoros Diasakos from Greece and Suzi Novak from the United States.

As part of the preparations that spring, the Kennedy School organized a symposium in which both Lebanese and Israeli students were brought together to debate the two-decade ongoing Israeli occupation of the south of Lebanon. At the time, there were some signals of Israel's withdrawal, but nothing firm. The debate was meant to highlight the issues and concerns of both nations. It was an intense but civil debate, in which the Israeli side argued that security had to be guaranteed before any withdrawal could take place. The Lebanese side, which I was on, argued that the occupation of the South was causing insecurity. If Israel withdrew from its illegal occupation, then it had nothing to worry about.

At the end of the debate, the Israeli student leader, a retired air force pilot, closed his side's argument by saying that he had had "The pleasure of flying his fighter jet over that beautiful country and feeling sorry for it, wishing that if security were to be guaranteed by the Lebanese that Israel would be happy to exit." In my closing rebuttal, I replied, "Yes, I may have seen my Israeli counterpart's plane up there, but cannot say I had the same degree pleasure, being on the bomb-receiving end. It is my hope that Israel's illegal occupation and necessary exit be immediate and unconditioned on any devised pre-condition. And if, God forbid, cross-border security proves to be as hazardous as is being claimed, I'm sure it'll give my honorable colleague an excuse to enjoy some more of his flying!"

The truth of the matter was little did any of us know that withdrawal would transpire so precipitously thereafter. A mere handful of weeks later, on May 24, 2000, and shortly before my Harvard team was set to travel to Lebanon, Israel unilaterally withdrew from the South.

To a Lebanese and Arab American who had been raised in a war-torn region and where being on the losing side seemed to be the only constant, this was no ordinary historical event. It was a defining moment that would become etched like no other. For once, I had good reason to be proud of my Lebanese heritage. I became filled with emotion and a desire to visit the very places that had just been liberated. I couldn't wait to learn from and share in the happiness of my fellow countrymen who had heroically freed themselves and the nation of unjust occupation. A few days later I would get that chance.

Travelling all over Lebanon that summer would prove to be a great source of erudition. It inspired me to write and share my experience with those not so fortunate to be there. My colleagues and I stayed at the American University of Beirut. Our dorm rooms in the Penrose Building were quite basic but had top-floor views overlooking the Mediterranean providing us spectacular fireball sunsets—something I rarely missed. Afterwards, I often got down to writing about my daily experiences. These experiences ranged from the trivial conversation to detailed analytical study; for during our stay we managed to interview ministers, leaders, politicians, academicians, researchers, and members of society at large. Interestingly, two trends emerged.

First, somewhat counter-intuitively, data was quite abundant. Everywhere I looked, there were economic, social, and technological data. It was quite extraordinary; and the challenge became much more so sifting through the volumes of data than simply finding it. This was a pleasant surprise and so was the fact that people in general were quite open to providing us with whatever data we asked for—even at the highest of levels. At OMSAR (the Lebanese Ministry of administrative reform), I recall its director, Raymond Khoury, providing us with valuable survey results for the state of technological ubiquity in the country based on a nationwide Y2K assessment. At the Ministry of Economy, Minister Nasser Saidi shared insight into Lebanon's trade policy and accords and provided us detailed trade data. At the Ministry of Finance, Jihad Azzour (who would later become the minister of finance) shared detailed information as to the debt and the action being taken to keep the budgets under control. During several interviews held at his offices in Beirut, Fouad Sinyora, who was the former minister of finance and out of government at the time (He would later become prime minister upon the assassination of Hariri) shared important insight into the post-war reconstruction period and the implementation of important tax reforms such as VAT and Customs. As a controversial figure in Lebanon who was often ridiculed for his tax policies, I found Minister Sinyora quite open to criticism and hard questioning. More importantly, I appreciated the fact that he preferred to base his argument on facts and figures.

Equally interesting as meeting these government officials, was meeting people in the field from different parts of Lebanon. In the North, we visited the Akkar region and were shown around by my friend Paul Salem. In the Shouf Mountains, we visited towns and got to see the revamping of certain municipalities. In the South, we visited Sidon and Tyre and got to see redeployed schools and repaired highways. In the Bekaa, we drove around noticing the stark contrast between the under-developed areas surrounding the world famous Roman ruins. One evening, as I attended an Italian opera concert held inside the ruins, I recall wondering what all those people outside of the walls of the temple were thinking. Did the music festival mean anything to them? Was it another reminder of how unjust the Lebanese state had been towards such a large swathe of its population?

Studying the country and its data more closely over the next three months would slowly temper my emergent national pride as a second thought trend emerged. With parts of the nation moving forward at dizzying speeds with manifestations of modernization and wealth; I could not help but see clearly that other portions were entrenched in poverty, downtrodden, and forgotten. And yet, depending on who we spoke to, different versions of the truth emerged. Notwithstanding the abundance of data, people we talked to saw things in different ways and seemingly were uninterested in what was going on in other parts of their nation. Unfortunately, at the governing level, policy decisions were being applied in an equally kaleidoscopic manner, with a chasm emerging between pubic need, politics, and policy—all potentially leading to an ever-worsening socio-economic situation.

And so during that summer, it dawned on me that the nation was not one and same; but rather an odd and uncomfortable agglomeration of statelets, each with its own history, ideology, and vision. Having liberated itself from formidable external foes, the country was still very much imprisoned in a tragic past and heading towards a parsimonious future. How long could such a nation sustain its salient geopolitical successes, while social and economic divides blatantly and stubbornly gnawed away at its very existence? I wondered…

Tour of liberation (June 2000)

Catching a cab in front of the American University of Beirut (AUB), I really had one thing in mind: I wanted to go to the south to see the recently liberated Lebanese lands. I did not have a map. I rarely carried one. Maybe it was because it made me feel less at home than I actually considered myself. Then again, where is home to many in my generation that had to leave during the war starting lives elsewhere?

I had planned and re-planned for this trip to the South before leaving the States. However, when it actually came time for it, I found myself quite ill prepared. I was accompanied by my Harvard colleague, Theo, which made the trip more comfortable. What was important to me was going there. Anything else really did not matter whatever I ended up seeing. Full of pride and expectations, I was heading to my beloved South on a tour of liberation.

I don't know why I had gotten attached to Lebanon's south. I mean, I really have no direct links. My family is partly from Tripoli in the North and from Beirut. Perhaps it was an emotional link, which had developed over the years with southerners whom I had met and found to be very warm, hospitable, and authentic. Perhaps it was a nationalistic one, seeing the people suffer and yet bravely resist the Israeli occupation. They had toiled year after another, blood drop after another to get back their land. It was a classic case of David and Goliath: The South in the face of the formidable Israeli Defense Forces. Town after town standing up against occupation injustices. The lone resistance fighter on a selfless mission against an Israeli Merkava tank.

It is within this context that I felt I had to see the South and experience the Lebanese accomplishment with my own eyes.

Beaufort Castle (June 2000)

The road to Beaufort Castle went through Nabatiyeh, one of the larger inland southern towns. The roads were surprisingly good; and the villages themselves, relatively orderly and clean. I had been told the South was beautifully green, and I was not disappointed with many olive, banana, and citric farms scattered around. The buildings and houses were also a surprise as many were architected using Mediterranean motifs—red brick roofs and limestone for siding. It seems many of the wealthy people that had emigrated from the South had constructed themselves elegant houses and villas—even while the land was still under Israeli occupation highlighting their belief of their ultimate victory and their families' inevitable return.

As we began our ascent to Beaufort Castle, one starts to appreciate military strategy and military advantage. While it is said that Beaufort Castle was built as long ago as Roman biblical time, not much is known before it was captured by the Crusaders in the early 12th century. And yet almost a millennium later, having exchanged hands to the likes of Saladin, the Knights of Templar, the Mamluks, Ottomans, and French, it still commanded strategic military prominence even to a modern aerial power such as Israel. The mountain atop which it sits overlooks most of the South and a large portion of north eastern Israel and the Golan heights. The mountain itself is steep and arid unlike the plains around it, leading me to believe it was razed by the Israelis for security reasons.

As we drove on, I was constantly wondering how courageous the Lebanese resistance must have been to go up against such an impregnable modernized fortress in what was obviously—even to a military layman such as myself—an impossible mission. How could they have done this? As if to answer my question, many a small flag were scattered on the road leading to the castle. I was later told each signified the place of fallen resistance fighters.

Once we reached the peak, remnants of Israel's military presence became more apparent. To my pleasant surprise, reports that the castle had been blown-up were ill-founded. The barracks around the castle were the ones actually aerially bombed by the Israelis to render them unusable, but the historical monument itself was minimally damaged.

We walked inside and around the castle. On the inside it is quite large but dark. We were told that there is a secret passage that led all the way down the mountain to the river. Trying to find it, we got lost and found ourselves climbing up and down Israeli tube metal staircases within the barracks. I wasn't very keen on this part of the journey as my mind kept imagining myself being blown up by some mine or unexploded bomb.

When we finally found our way back, I was pumped up having practically gone through a military drill. I urged our driver to take us to the next place in our liberation tour: The Khayyam Prison.

Ali Himmadeh's Khayyam Prison (June 2000)

It looked and sounded like a place straight out of a Western movie. Wind was blowing from all sides—as if on a mission to vacuum clean the place of its sad history. Windows of abandoned posts incessantly screeched open only to come to a thundering close. This was the notorious Khayyam prison, the one that had been liberated by the village people and the resistance a few weeks earlier in a peaceful and yet heroic stance against Israel's left over proxies in Lebanon, the South Lebanon Army (SLA). The scene of the liberation had been described to me by a reporter friend and eye witness...

She recalled that as news began emerging that the Israeli army was retreating from the different areas in the South, she and one of her colleagues at the Agence France Press got a call to travel from Beirut to the south and to report on what was going on. What she witnessed was extraordinary:

Massive popular convoys who were defying government safety warning and heading south were already lining the streets and highways. Once in the South, the resistance, villagers, and returning refugees began marching into each of the villages being vacated by the Israelis—including Khayyam, which my friend recalled took on even more significance. Central to this town was the regional Khayyam prison utilized by the Israelis for two decades. It was located at the edge of the town on a small hill.

As the liberators reached the doors of the Khayyam prison, the left over proxy SLA soldiers threatened to shoot at the crowd. One of the liberators took the lead and asked the guards to leave in peace because they had no way of defending themselves against the crowds. The prison guards did not agree at first. However, the crowd peacefully appealed to the senses of the guards and began pressing against the gates. Soon, the guards began feeling the pressure. A short while afterwards they readily accepted to leave, if they could be brought a car and assured of an exit route. Their wish attained, they left the prison to the liberators.

In the meantime, the Lebanese prisoners locked inside their cells did not know what was happening outside. When they heard the screaming and the shouting, they mistook the liberators for Israelis coming to hurt or kill them. "Allahou Akbar" (God is great) calls started being heard all over the prison as the prisoners awaited their moment of deliverance. They soon realized, however, that they were actually being liberated. Village people and the resistance scrambled for anything they could find to break the cell door locks open. Rocks, steel bars, anything they could lay their hands on. Tears flowing on both sides of the prison bars made the work harder, but also pushed the liberators to work harder. Finally, the prison doors broke open to those that had not seen liberty in many years. The prisoners were raised on the shoulders of the liberators...

My mind would recall this story over and over again as we now headed to the village of Khayyam. The road leading to the village showed little if any signs of its notoriety. In fact, it could have been just any other road leading to this or that part of any Lebanese village. But it didn't. It led to the village, which housed Khayyam prison, a prison that had witnessed more than two decades of Israeli injustice over Lebanon and in particular the South. We drove up to a parking lot where a soft spoken young man wearing a yellow Hezbollah cap and a shy smile guided us to where we could park the car. Once parked, we walked uphill for about half a kilometer to get to the entrance of the prison where there were a few men sitting unobstructively on the side. Perhaps they could have been just boys; but their bushy beards and defiant demeanor exposed them as men. I asked to take a photo with them; they did not accept but urged me to walk in and take pictures of the prison instead.

Walking into the prison gates, to the left were the guard rooms. The liberators had made sure that the names of the guards that had been on duty were posted on a cardboard, lest they be forgotten. Alas, they were mostly Lebanese names. The Israelis as many others before them had made sure the locals did their dirty work for them. At the center of the prison entrance, there was a courtyard in which there were two five meter high concrete posts connected at the top by a concrete beam with protruding steel hooks—no doubt used for hangings or some other torture method. On this day, however, hanging on a rope from the top was a dummy with an Israeli uniform surrounded at the base by barbed wire. Due to the howling wind, the dummy was circling around with the clothes being gnawed at by the barbed wire. Further on in the courtyard, there was another gate. This one lead to the prisoners' quarters. There were four quarters, one of which was for women. It was there that I met Ali Himmadeh.

Ali was a short man, probably in his mid-thirties. He had a light beard on and wore jeans and a denim shirt. He exhibited an easy and peaceful demeanor as he explained to visitors Khayyam's story. He approached me and Theo asking if we cared for a tour, explaining that he and some five other ex-inmates had taken it upon themselves to explain to visitors what had been going on inside the prison during the previous two decades.

He began by explaining that he had been incarcerated in 1992 because he had refused to join the SLA. It was not until 1998 that he had been released in a prisoner exchange. Ali guided us inside the first quarter and through a long thin corridor. On the right side of the corridor, there were dark cells. Each was about two meters wide, 10 meters long and 3 meters high. He explained that until 1995, the prison had only had isolated cells; but the Red Cross had made the Israelis open up the rooms to these dimensions for humanitarian reasons. Thus each of these rooms which housed some six or seven inmates had been six or seven cells prior to 1995. The rooms were dimly lit with a damp smell. At the end of each room, there was a bathroom that seemed to offer no reasonable amount of privacy. Food was given through the cell bars and included meager portions: one egg with a piece of bread in the morning and potatoes for lunch. Ali explained how drinking water used to be bargained for. Anytime there was a shortage, the prisoners would go on hunger strikes. On this issue, he grinned, they usually won with more drinking water delivered. On many other issues, he said they were not so fortunate.

I asked Ali how it was the first few days in prison for him. He explained that the first 28 days were usually spent between solitary confinement and interrogation. During the day, they would interrogate them, and then they would transfer them to their solitary cell. Sometimes, if answers were not obtained, they would use electric currents applied through the fingers, or they would use belts and other leather items to lash at the prisoners. If they still received no information, then they would take them to a room with what appeared to be another prisoner. The other prisoner would be an undercover agent and would try to extract information by telling them some made-up story of his own resistance activities in the hope that they would fall in the trap by admitting some of their own experiences or information. If this method did not work either, then they would take them to the 'Amoud (the post), which was strategically placed between the quarters. The prisoner would then have his or her head covered with a thick blue head cover, and then would be hung from the post with police-like hand cuffs—feet not touching the ground. Threats, abuses, and beatings heard by all would follow. Ali told us he remembered that the jailers once had been watching some boxing match on television and a prison mate was blindfolded and hanging from the post. As soon as the match was over, the jailers came out and started practicing the punches that they had learnt watching the game. "I know of five prisoners who died on this post over the years," Ali sighed.

As we returned into the quarters moving along the corridors joining the cells, many people in the small group began dropping out either because it was too claustrophobic, or they could not bear the stench. I tend to think, however, that they simply could not take in any more of this uncensored and ugly reality. It would get worse as the tour progressed, for then; Ali guided us to the solitary confinement quarters. In this part of the prison, cells were barely a meter wide, a meter long, and a meter and a half high. Sleeping could only be done in the sitting position. Mattresses and daylight were a luxury that many a prisoner did not receive; so were bathrooms, with buckets serving as convenient replacements. Prisoners could stay anywhere between one and twelve weeks in this type of confinement. In one of these rooms, Ali had stayed the first four weeks. He showed us the spot where he had etched his name using a nail that he had found by accident under his mattress. He went on to explain that his mattress was an inch thick. Only after Red Cross insistence in 1995, did the mattresses become about 8 centimeters in thickness.

By the end of the tour, I wanted to ask Ali a million other questions. I mean here was a man who had suffered a lot of injustice, and yet his demeanor showed not an iota of hatred. He seemed like a man at ease with a life that had served him a great injustice. I wanted to know why and how he managed to overcome his ordeal. I wanted to know how he felt about people who had robbed him of a decade of his life. But I also knew that he needed to share his and Khayyam's story with the many other groups which were arriving. So, I decided to simply ask for a photo.

As he turned his back and walked away, I could not help but think of the sacrifices that people such as Ali Himmadeh have had to face on behalf of Lebanon. I also could not help but admire the courage that he and the other men had mustered in coming back to this prison to tell their story in its ugly truth, within the very walls that had tortured them for so many years. These are brave men. These are good men. They are Lebanon's true heroes.

Fatimah's Gate (June 2000)

Upon leaving Khayyam, I was in a rather solemn mood; for it is a place whose sadness and pain hangs in the air. And yet, I was also filled with pride for the South and its people. They had resisted an occupation and ultimately gotten rid of the Israelis from their land. As if needing to assert this fact, I urged the driver on to Bawwabet Fatimah (Fatimah's gate), perhaps the most known Lebanese-Israeli border points. It is a mere 2 kilometers east of Khayyam in the town of KfarKilla.

Several thoughts struck me as I walked along the border towards the Fatimah gate. The first is that this border reminded me of several I had seen in different parts of the world. Like those, it was filled with merchants and peddlers trying to sell all kinds of memorabilia. They were quite busy. Another thought was the awkward fact that there was no military presence at the Lebanese side of the border. Knowing that the army had not yet taken over, I had at least expected to see a few Lebanese resistance fighters. There were none in sight. How utterly wrong all those Israeli security fear mongers had been. The Lebanese resistance actions spoke louder than any words: Having accomplished their goal of getting the Israelis out of Lebanon, they were satisfied with a quiet border. This led me to the final thought that struck me and it was the business as usual attitude of the Lebanese sauntering at our side of the border. I could have sworn these same people could have been walking along the Corniche carrying their masbaha (beads) and admiring a typical Mediterranean sunset. There were two or three men throwing stones at the Israeli border post, which also seemed unmanned. I must admit that I also had the urge of carrying a stone or better yet an old shoe and throwing it to make a statement if anything. I held back avoiding giving the other side the pleasure of an excuse they were desperately seeking. I believe this restraint to be the same decision being carried out by the Lebanese resistance—a wise one indeed.

Driving back to Beirut that evening, I looked back on my tour of liberation and was filled with mixed emotions. On the one hand, I was filled with happiness for and pride in our South, its people, and their determination through resistance to retrieve what was rightfully theirs. On the other hand, I was also filled with sorrow and pain for the suffering that the region and its people had to endure through all these years. I was all the more humbled in the knowledge that the people of the South practically did it on their own against very heavy odds. And yet, in place of intoxicating themselves with congratulations upon their victory, they extended their arms to the entire Lebanese nation to embrace victory as a national one. This act of magnanimity is without precedent in our nation and not to be taken lightly or picked at, no matter what cynics might say. To me, it is a sign of rejuvenated hope. It is an indirect way of saying that ours is a beautiful country to be cherished and held onto in every one of its corners. It is another way of saying; Lebanon is a gift to all the Lebanese, lest it be forgotten from time to time.

The Lebanese resistance, the least endowed of our nation, the least educated, and the least privileged has taught not only Lebanon, but the Arab world and the world at large an important lesson: Even in this day and age, might is not always right. Rather, right can muster might. It is the duty of Lebanon to honor this accomplishment and keep its spirit alive for posterity.

Downtown Beirut (July 2000)

Every generation tends to romanticize its "good old days". No better an example than in our beloved Lebanon. Our fathers always talk about the good old days of Lebanon—usually followed by a description of the grandiose center of Beirut in the 1960s, its hotels, and its souks. Of course, they quickly add, that the current center of Beirut is but a replica of what used to be; and that it should have been done the "old way" to reflect our true history and culture.

To me, this line of argument is faulty, unfairly selfish, and counter-productive. I ask myself, what is this "old way" that they talk about? Could it really have been as good as they say? After all, haven't numerous others claimed that this "old way" was partially responsible for leading our country down the path of catastrophic civil strife? How good could it have been when it led to their own children not being able to play in peace, go to school in tranquility, nor sleep in their beds? Surely, our fathers recognize that not everything the "old way" was as they currently romanticize it to have been.

I recognize that our generation should feel a certain degree of sympathy towards the older generation for all the years and opportunities that they lost as a result of the war. After all, if the older generation wishes to engage itself in wishful thinking about the "old ways", reminisce about the past, and imagine what the future could have been, then this exercise in and of itself is surely harmless. Our generation should bear along, as we hope our own children will one day bear along listen to our "good old days" spiel. Nevertheless, our generation should also recognize that in no way are we liable to be held responsible—let alone ideologically hostage—for the war or its consequences. Furthermore, if the older generation's thought exercise were to become a basis for *returning* to the "old ways", then our generation should immediately refute it.

That is why when I walk the streets of downtown Beirut, I really do not care if it is referred to as a Saudi replica, a Hariri pet project, a middle class rip-off, a cheap imitation, a nothing-like-the-old thing, or any other name it has been called. What I truly care about is the reality that I see with my own eyes. It is the reality of seeing a kaleidoscope of Phoenician, Roman, Arab, Ottoman, and Lebanese history erected side-by-side in uniquely Lebanese elegance and style. It is the reality of the narrow cobblestone walkways running between renovated buildings lit from below with multi-colored floodlights. It is the reality of evening promenades among hundreds of fellow Lebanese from all walks of life in an area that a decade earlier had been laid to waste and forgotten. It is the reality of sitting in outdoor cafes and enjoying the food and the traditional 'argileh' (Hubble-bubble), and—if a decent opponent be present—a game of 'Tawleh' (Backgammon). It is the reality of enjoying live music and being surrounded with people singing and laughing with little care in the world. I simply refuse to allow this crystal clear reality—albeit imperfect with some controversial decisions made along the way—to be blurred or distorted by those attached to a shadow of the past or delirious about some oasis of a long gone future.

As harsh as it may sound, our generation no longer cares about the "old ways" or the old Lebanon for that matter. Our generation prepaid a hefty deposit and is desperate to put the past behind. Our generation wants and deserves to construct its own images and memories of the emerging Lebanon without needing to be constantly reminded, let alone restrained by "old ways" indelibly attached to painful memories. Our generation wants and needs a fresh start. Downtown Beirut—although by no means the solution to all Lebanese tribulations—is a big leap forward. It is a signal of potentially good things to come and gives us the sense that Lebanon is no longer a faraway dream to be remembered occasionally through Fairuz tunes. It is a reality, and it is back!

As our generation steps up to its responsibilities, alas the law of nature beckons the older generation to step aside. It is our hope that they do it graciously and in good spirits. As we prepare to grapple and grope with many a prominent issue facing Lebanon, it is our hope that our fathers will not criticize or hinder our energetic drive, but rather, support our decisions, and understand our potential mistakes. The time has come for our generation to start building its own children's past and future. The time has come for us to be proud of everything we are by showing the world what we can and want to be.

Two sights no eyes should see (July 2000)

It was a hot and humid Sunday afternoon; and I was taking a jog along the Corniche of Beirut. I stopped to catch my breath and catch a view of my beloved Mediterranean. As I stood and looked out to sea, I had a unique experience. For at this instant, each of my two eyes were seeing two different and contrasting images. One was an upscale and exclusive private beach; while the other was a bubbling makeshift public beach not 30 yards to the right. It was a contradiction staring me in the eyes. It deeply bothered me.

The first image I was eyeing was a sheltered private beach club hotel with a small marina in the Ras Beirut area. Were it not for its fancy name and its image as being the place where the wealthier crowd moved and shook, many other a private beach no doubt would have surpassed its rocky beach. And yet over the past decade, this particular one had held its ground and become a status symbol in its own right. It was situated right off of the Corniche, which is a three-kilometer strip that shoulders the sea, giving Beiruti saunterers a spectacular view of the Mediterranean—especially during sunsets. During the war, this hotel had become bare and run down. Its beach had been left unattended for a long time. At the end of the civil war, however, it was revamped; with its beach concealed behind large blue vinyl sheets hoisted slantingly upwards and tied to metal posts so as to keep eyeing Corniche walkers from looking within. To get in to its beach club, one needed to pay a hefty membership fee.

The other beach to the right appeared to be open to the public. Geologically speaking, this beach seemed to be just as un-endowed as its neighbor to its left. However, it had not had the benefit of any recent facelift nor a marina—just a small government posted-sign that warned swimmers to watch their step; for to get down to this public beach from the Corniche, one had to descend a steep 10-foot rusted metal staircase. Once down, there were no seating or fancy umbrellas. People just sat around on their towels or wooden chairs on top of the rocks and played backgammon, smoking their argileh. Meanwhile, their kids were swimming, laughing, and enjoying themselves without a care in the world.

I had seen many such contrasts throughout my life especially in South America, where I had worked and lived for some time. As unfair as it seemed, it was not a strange sight for my eyes to see. So, I did not quite understand at first what it was that was bothering me. Surely, it wasn't some first world idealist view that was projecting itself onto the apparent Lebanese chasm I was witnessing. It had to be something else.

The next afternoon, I happened to be in the company of a group of executives, one of whom was a Lebanese manager of a multi-national auditing firm. He had a sophisticated aura about him. The conversation turned to Lebanon's development. The man seemed to have few verbal inhibitions, and spent the better part of the discussion nagging about current conditions and adamantly against any form of taxation or government intervention, adding that a certain portion of the Lebanese population have "always been poor and will always be poor".

Now, had this person been uneducated or mentally incapable, an easy explanation for his opinions would have been easy to muster up. However, he was supposedly a graduate from the US and had lived and worked in Canada—a place where one can fairly assume such chasms and inequality manifestations are almost non-existent. So, I could not understand why he seemed to insist on accepting them in his own nation. Did he not see or understand that most developing and developed countries do have a need for public goods—be they public parks, highway systems, social security, education or even defense—all of which are paid for through one form of taxation or another. Canada's highways were not built by the largesse of its rich classes any more than its national parks, medical or educational systems. It was built by the hard earned taxes of its people. Prosperous countries like Holland literally created their homeland out of swamps, and most of the work was funded by the state taxing its citizenry in an economic tide that raised everyone's boat, so to speak.

Surely, men like him understood that most developed countries in North America and Europe and developing ones in Latin America and South Asia have worked hard to create relatively equitable systems that have given their people fair settings in which they could live and prosper. Surely, he knew that one way to alleviate social distress—and the potential of civil hostilities—is through state policies that support those less privileged through education, health care support, work programs, and even income redistribution. Furthermore, I assumed that, as an accountant, surely he understood that Lebanon, which is not as endowed with oil reserves as some of its neighbors, would not be able to go ad-infinitum without balancing its direly needed social expenditures through revenues such as taxes. Surely, fresh in his memory must be the fact that part of the civil war was caused because of inequitable and shortsighted economic policies that refused to acquiesce to growing mass disenchantment.

Unfortunately, he didn't seem to have a clue. I reasoned he either didn't *want* to get it or worse yet he simply didn't care. If there are many others like him, what future could this nation expect for itself? This bothers me.

Sheltered from reality (August 2000)

After some reflection, more questions began surfacing in my mind. Why was there such stark economic disparity in Lebanon to begin with? Is this the Lebanon that always was? Is it what always has to be? What has the government been doing to rectify the situation? Could Lebanon ever see itself out of this predicament? How? I set about trying to find out.

It turns out that economic disparity and poverty in Lebanon have indeed been a fact of life since independence. In the 1960s and 1970s, Lebanon already had widening income disparity with GINI coefficients (a disparity indicator) upward of 0.55—closer to high-inequality nations such as Mexico (0.53) and Nigeria (0.63) than more equitably-distributed countries such as the US, Japan, South Korea, and Europe (all around 0.3). In fact, right before the civil war, some 5% of the Lebanese population controlled more than 90% of the country's GDP, leaving more than 40% of the population in an utterly deprived state in rural areas such as Akkar, Bekaa, and the South.

During the war, because of hyperinflation and the eventual devaluation of the Lebanese Lira, the situation would get even worse. As a result, much of the Lebanese middle class was wiped out. Those more fortunate immigrated. And today, even though the per capita GDP in Lebanon stands above US$5,000, in real terms it constitutes only half of what it used to be in 1974, leading World Bank and UNDP reports to point to more than 50% of the Lebanese population living under the poverty line.

Half a century after independence, poor areas continue to be concentrated around Beirut, in Akkar, the Bekaa, Hermel, and the South with many still lacking basic amenities such as water and sewage, electricity, proper public schooling, and health facilities.

Why did this come about in the first place? In a nutshell, politically they were due to systemic deficiencies including political hegemony with regional considerations trumping national ones. Leadership was shortsighted but rarely held accountable because of a frail democratic system based on confessional rather than national allegiance. From an economic standpoint, it was due to economic activity concentration in the urban areas—specifically in Beirut, disregard for certain high-employment sectors of the economy such as agriculture, and lack of economic development plan executions. From a social perspective, it is the result of social injustice where certain regions, classes, or sects in the country were practically left to fend for themselves with little help from the central government—be it in terms of education, health services, or poverty alleviation.

This does not mean the government over the past five decades did not know of the problem or try to do anything about it. In fact, the government did try to implement certain economic development work aimed at eradicating social ills such as poverty and economic disparity. However, some plans were ill conceived—as in the Camille Chamoun era in the 1950s. Others were not executed fully—as in the Fouad Shehab and Helou eras in the 1960s. Some were refuted because of political pressures—as in the Franjiyeh eras in the 1970's. And some never had the chance because of the ensuing civil war situation—as in the Sarkis and Gemayel eras in the 1980s.

In the 1990s, the government was able to accomplish some projects. Contrary to popular belief that all post-war spending went on futile reconstruction efforts, the government's expenditures totaled around $15 billion—*grosso modo* 35% on infrastructure projects, 32% on military expenditures and 33% on social spending. In terms of infrastructure, the government was able to renew highway links to the South and North and build better road networks within and around the capital Beirut, the Bekaa. Ports were re-habilitated in Sidon, Beirut, and Tripoli. A state of the art national telephone network with 1 million fixed lines was installed, and massive work was deployed on water, sewage, and electricity utility improvements.

The military spend was primarily on army rehabilitation, retirement to two generations of military officers, and payoff to the civil war militias. And in terms of social spending, it was focused on the revamping of some 700 public-schools, compensation for the displaced, poor and middle-income housing subsidies, health services, as well as social security.

Notwithstanding the many criticisms and corruption allegations, and considering the on-going regional conflicts, one may objectively argue that the post-war governments and our fledgling democracy—even though far from perfect—have delivered some obvious results. However, with so many more things to do—and assuming for a moment that most of the expenditures were and continue to be inevitable—the real problem is going to be how to fund these government expenditures if they are not matched with equal revenues. The government has begun issuing debt in order to finance the difference—technically called the budget deficit. By the end of the civil war, in 1992, the government had a debt close to US$3 billion; but by 2000, it had grown to US$22 billion. The government now finds that more than 80% of its expenditures are going towards interest payments and salaries. So, it has its hands tied when it comes to further spending on any new projects—let alone development projects to tackle poverty or income disparity alleviation.

In the meantime, the highly ambitious Lebanese citizen expecting to see a transformation of the country's 50-year ills (close to 20 of which were in civil war and unrest) in less than a decade has had a rude awakening only managing to express frustrations through nagging or lethargy. For the few with the means, there are always the cocky attitudes, the luxury cars, the ear plugged cell phones, and the fancy beach escapades. For the vast majority, it is growing frustration.

Is Lebanon beyond the point of no return? Is it doomed to economic inequality, social injustice, and erupting cycles of violence? Is it as some say it has always been? Can anything be done to rectify the situation? As bad as it might seem to be, I do not believe the situation is yet a lost cause— that is, as long as the Lebanese can get their act together when it comes to fundamental issues such as long-term vision and planning, hard-work in execution, accountability for the government, and cooperation and trust fostering initiatives within civil society.

The Lebanese like to show their *joi de vivre* attitude. While there is nothing wrong with this and life sometimes requires some levity, alas it cannot be all fun. In a young family's life, the occasional weekend outing is harmless—and arguably necessary to maintains one's sanity—if careful planning is maintained, supported by hard-work, education for the children, proper housing, and proper health care the rest of the time. Throughout this time, for its own long term good, the family is creating social and professional ties that are based on honesty, mutual trust, and cooperation. In the meantime, the family has to be paying its dues; and always balancing it by receiving benefits in return. And at the end of the road, the family hopes to be able to retire in peace and find happiness be it through gardening, grandchildren, wealth, fame... Is a nation much different? Is it not just a bigger family? How then, could a family expect to be successful—let alone happy—with almost half of its members living in poverty and receiving no proper education, basic amenities, or hope of a better future let alone a tranquil retirement?

Lebanon can no longer afford to be sheltered from this reality. Those hoisted vinyl sheets delineating society will once again come crumbling down over the heads refusing to see these truths, as indeed they have many times in the past. It is time for the Lebanese to face up to some of the unfolding and ugly truths. Fortunately, the country is small—and everybody is endowed with brains and an even bigger mouth! The problems are already known—many of the potential solutions as well. The Lebanese are hard-working people, and have brains—so why not a heart to go along with it? What are we waiting for? Whatever the solutions, let them be adopted. If it means economic development by helping the lesser privileged, so be it. If it means growth by fostering the private sector or privatizing state institutions with proper controls, so be it. And if it means heavier taxation, then let it be the ugly pill that needs to be swallowed to relieve the nation of its ills and instead provide a civilized nation's education, health services, and tranquil retirement for its elderly.

At times it seems to me that fear truly has had no meaning in this land ever since ancestors several millennia ago ventured into a blue unknown seeking better livelihood. So if it means all the above solutions and more; the Lebanese should say "By God bring it on!" With the right mix of sacrifice, hard work, love of nation, and patience, they can and they will make it to the benefit of all and not just the few!

This little something (August 2000)

"Do you think the Lebanese middleman role has become obsolete?" I asked him.

"No," he answered, "it's just beginning".

The answer took me completely by surprise. I had asked this question to many other academicians and economic experts and most had provided me much gloomier scenarios, sighting the Internet, globalization, and Arab advances as having rung the death knell of the age-old Lebanese comparative-advantage. Did he know what he was talking about or was he seeing things in a totally different light? I wondered.

Noticing my bewilderment, he added, "You see, we Lebanese continue to have what others don't. It's *this little something*," he moved his long fingers in the air as if trying to catch some imaginary particles in order to demonstrate to me what he meant. "This little something," he continued, "cannot be replaced or replicated by computers, the Internet, or others in our region."

I had been in the company of a prominent Lebanese ex-minister from Tripoli who was a very close friend of my family. His words often carried weight with me; and on this occasion, I found myself carrying them around for days trying to decipher their full meaning. What could this *little something* be? What was its source? How did it practically manifest itself? Why did he seem to see it and not others? If it did indeed exist, would it be enough to carry Lebanon forward? Questions, questions, and more questions... It merits more reflection.

So, how best to describe this *little something*? The next day we were heading to the Dog River. It would give me a chance to find out. The river sources in Mount Lebanon and works its way through the mountains ending at its mouth in the Mediterranean Sea some twenty kilometers north of Beirut. The river is famous in ancient history as having been an agreed-upon delineation of territory between the Egyptian forces of the great Ramses II and his Anatolian counterparts, the Hittites in the 14th century BC.

Driving from Beirut along the coastline, it took us about half an hour to reach the mouth of the river. Once passed a landmark tunnel, the driver made a sharp right turn and parked the car by the side of the road. When we got out, the almost dry river was positioned slightly to the left flowing rather exhaustedly at the base of a steep slope towards the sea. It could have been just any other Mediterranean scene. Only, it wasn't. At the bottom of the slope to our right and etched into the mountain were several large upright rectangular marble signs and monuments carefully spaced out. We drew closer to try reading the signs. They proved to be signs left by every invading army that had gone through this region from Egyptians, Babylonians, Greeks, Persians, Romans, all the way to the British and French. It seemed all had felt the need to leave a trace of their presence. Had they? Could this dizzying history and civilizational center point have forced within the inhabitants an infinite capacity to adapt and an invincible nature? Could this be part of our *little something*?

The next morning, I woke up to the sound of the Muezzin. It was a peculiar voice with a beautiful tune that I had not heard before. Music and religion sometimes mix to memorable effect. It would be a good start to a busy day, for later on we were going to meet with the president of Balamand University in the Koura Mountains.

Koura is in the north of Lebanon some five kilometers south of Tripoli. The area is famous for its olive oil—actually a Koura gentleman confided to me that the only thing better than Koura olive oil are the Koura women—an interesting comparison in and of itself! It took us about ninety minutes to get to Koura from Beirut. The drive along the coastline was hot and humid, until the cab began his ascent towards the university. Once there, the view and freshness of the atmosphere changed noticeably.

Entering into his office, our host greeted us jovially. Dr. Salem was taller than I had envisioned him; and he stood upright emitting an air of authority; and yet, he was not over-imposing. Rather, he came across as quite amicable; and his smile—usually followed by a giddy laugh—reminded one of schoolmates. I had read his writings of his service as Lebanon's foreign minister during the war years and had found them to be engaging, moderate, and patriotic. It had not been an easy nor safe job.

Looking around his office, however, I was surprised by the many religious icons hanging on the walls. "Oh, oh..." I thought to myself, "Had confessional regression claimed yet another victim from moderate Lebanese intellectuals?" What followed, however, would set my fears to rest, for Dr. Salem did not attempt to hide his religious affiliation. As a matter of fact, he did not try to hide anything. He was a man who was quite comfortable with his Christianity and yet felt neither threat from nor hatred towards any other Lebanese sect—be it Islamic or Christian. If anything, he seemed quite knowledgeable, understanding, and I would venture to say appreciative of some of its legacies. To him Lebanon simply could not exist without one or the other religious pillar; and Lebanon's future depended on what he curiously called a "concordance between the voice of the Muezzin and the tolling of church bells".

That afternoon, having returned to my apartment, I heard the prayers of that same Muezzin again. This time, though, they were serendipitously accompanied by church bells. I smiled. Could positive elements coming from religious diversity be part of the *little something*?

A few days later, I met Abu Hussein, a tall dark toned man in his fifties. He was a cab driver in his mid-fifties from the Bekaa. He told me he had conceived some 7 children, 3 of which are triplets. I asked him how he managed to keep ends meet. He said he taught in the mornings while in the afternoon had been working importing cars from Germany and reselling them in the local market. Due to recent governmental legislation, however, his business was brought to a halt; and so he was now driving a 'service' (taxi cab).

"Three of my kids are finishing their university degrees. One is doing medicine, the other in business, and I have a girl in agriculture," he said proudly.

"I admire your work ethic and persistence," I responded.

"Mister, let me tell you something," he answered, "Whatever work I have to do, my utmost priority and pride is seeing my kids through university. I refuse to beg like some people, and to me any kind of work is honorable."

To my pleasant surprise, it turns out Abu Hussein spoke English and German having lived in the States as well as in Germany during Lebanon's war years. Here was a man with one thing on his mind: working hard to give his kids education for a better future. He simply refused to sit home and complain. Could Abu Hussein's determination and belief in education be another part of *this little something*?

That same evening, I happened to go out with a group of friends to a place by the name of Vida y Libertad (Life and Liberty). The place is located in Kaslik and is decorated with a Che Guevara revolutionary motif. For a couple of hours, I was transported to Cuba with live Celia Cruz and Tito Puente salsa music. Anyone who has not experienced nightlife in Cuba might as well go to this place; for it's as close as you can get to the real thing without actually being under Fidel's wings. One member of our group happened to be a professor at AUB with a PhD from the MIT in the US. She spoke some five languages and jumped between one and the other as nimbly as she did between mambo and salsa dance steps.

"Now, what the heck is your story?" I asked her curiously.

Turns out she doesn't have any family from South America, but was simply intrigued with Latino spirit and passion—from halfway around the world! She has already been on missions to most of South America and was working on starting a foundation that would bring Latin American kids of Lebanese heritage to Lebanon. Does her passionate and adventurous spirit symbolize *this little something*?

How about Abu El Abed and Abu Steif, two folkloric Lebanese characters whose quotidian adventures and tribulations are meant to poke fun of the most basic flaws in the Lebanese character?—By the way, did you hear the latest one?

Surely, the above is but a sampling of Lebanese people and traits that do not do justice to the actual population. If anything, it under-represents the myriad of unique traits and experiences that Lebanon and the Lebanese have developed over the millennia. Nevertheless, it does serve to show that the Lebanese must have a *little something* that is special. People talk about the benefits of globalization, when it has been the modus operandi in this land for the past three thousand years dating back to Phoenician traders who navigated the Mediterranean and parts of the Atlantic? They talk about the clash of East and West. I invite people to visit Lebanon and see the beauty of its harmony. They talk about Lebanon missing the boat; I could have sworn a cruise ship was anchored yesterday in Beirut port full of European tourists! They talked, they talk, and they will continue to talk. Let them talk, whilst we learn, toil, and produce.

My friend must be right. Somehow the land that is now Lebanon over the centuries has managed to produce *this little something*—providing its people with a unique mix of East meets West adaptability, education, ambition, taste, and why not, a little *joi de vivre*.

Now, there are those who will, pinpoint as I have just done, the source of our *little something* by seeking the answers in the differences *within* the Lebanese! They are wasting their time and should be shunned. We have had as much successes as failures in all Lebanese communities, and the answer does not lie in their crescent or cross. Friends, the answer is staring us right in the face. This enigmatic source is non-other than Lebanon itself. Yes, it is the *one and only* Lebanon in the universe, with everything and everyone. Without it and without all the communities housed within it, we are but a distant concept. A dream. Without it, our *little something* risks evaporating in the air never to be retrieved. Without it, we are but a social security number, a chador, or a "Turco"[1].

For those who still carry doubts of who they are, hasn't the war given you a taste of what you thought would be better? And wasn't it bitter? The Lebanese, renowned for their salesmanship, never again should sell their country short. In the coming future, we should expect to be put to many tests. The offers will increasingly be many and will come in different shapes and forms. The better off Lebanon gets, the more offers are to be expected. They will come from the naïve, the mal intentioned, the envious, and the interested. They will come from near and from far. Whatever the source and whatever the offered price, it will always be cheap, for one indelibly has to wonder the priceless value of *this little something*.

Until the Lebanese understand—and explain to their children that *the little something* was not too long ago at the point of extinction, there is a risk that Lebanon's tragic history repeats itself. Instead, with time, persistence, patience, and cooperation, we can learn and then teach kids how to value Lebanon above everything else in the hope that it perpetuates this unique *little something*—dare I call it Lebanese Identity!

---

1 A "Turco" meaning "Turk" is a generic term used throughout Latin America to describe someone from Middle Eastern descent as most immigrants in the 19th and early 20th century carried Ottoman passports.

Section Two:
War In Iraq
(2003-2004)

SECTION TWO:
WAR IN IRAQ
(2003-2004)

On the morning of September 11th, 2001, I happened to be on a business trip to São Paulo in Brazil and was scheduled to travel back to the United States that very evening. Working on my computer in my hotel room that morning, I had little idea what was transpiring in the northern hemisphere. I barely noticed on TV, which was muted in the background, the pictures of the New York World Trade Center Towers. After a few minutes, I glimpsed on the screen some smoke rising from a building; and thought it was probably a fire of some sort. A few minutes later I looked again and noticed several fires were now raging from different parts of the building, which I discerned as New York's World Trade Center. Immediately it dawned on me that there was only one tower standing up!

I had been at the top of the North Tower a few years earlier in a technology event held at the Windows on the World restaurant complex. I recall it had been an impressive venue with a magnificent view of the entire Upper Bay including the Statue of Liberty and Ellis Island. That evening, the view had been all the more stunning with a memorable sunset that created a palette of colors and shades all over the bay. And now I was witnessing all hell breaking loose. As I turned on the volume, what I thought was some freak fire accident turned out to be a deliberate attack on the United States.

A few eternal moments later, as I watched the North tower come down, two things dawned on me. First, that the world would never be the same. It wasn't only walls that were falling; a global geopolitical status quo was falling with it and in front of the world's very eyes. And second, if this attack turned out to be linked to the Arab world, I feared there would be enormous repercussions.

Over the next few months my instincts would be confirmed. A group of Islamic fundamentalists pertaining to Al Qaeda had perpetrated the attacks. As a result, both Afghanistan and Iraq would be invaded by the United States in what would soon be coined as the Global War on Terror.

Since Al Qaeda had planned for and was operating from inside Afghanistan, abetted by the Taliban, most of the world did not seem to mind the United States' bombing and later invasion of Afghanistan in retaliation to the New York attacks. However, many later felt that the United States had no such justification or business in invading Iraq. Stalwart American allies in the West—the likes of France, Germany, and Belgium—vehemently opposed it. The United States countered by stating that the situation in the Middle East had become too threatening and had spilled onto its own shores. It could no longer be ignored; nor could the status quo of coexistence with menacing regimes such as Saddam be any longer maintained.

In the Middle East, I found that generally Arab sentiment tended to be that of indignation in what they saw as nothing but aggression led by cynical American geopolitics. 'It was the United States' way of controlling the region and sucking it dry of its oil,' was one of many such claims made—and perhaps for good reason. Saddam, like other numerous Arab dictators before him, had been supported by the West at one point or another; and some felt the minute he was no longer useful, he was deposed.

As an Arab American, I found that there was truth as well as error on the arguments from both sides. Regardless, I tended to see the debate a bit futile; for irrespective of who was right, the invasion itself was a game changer in that the United States had reversed almost a half century worth of support for regional dictators by deciding to once and for all get rid of one of its most notorious, Saddam Hussein. This in itself was momentous because it was not simply a move on the geopolitical chess board; in a way, it was an attempt to change the entire chessboard. It cemented the notion that things could never be the same regardless of whose argument was right or wrong.

And so my writings at the time were not so much to convince fellow Americans to occupy any more than it was to convince fellow Arabs to accept occupation. Rather, it was more about the next step—that of accepting events and moving on to something hopefully better for Iraq and the Arab region and of course the United States. This writing often provoked heated debate with colleagues in the United States as well as some in the region. While many were dubious of my arguments and questioned my optimism, the Lebanese English daily, The Daily Star, encouraged me by publishing several of my pieces. And while I cannot say whether or not it was supportive of my line of argument, at least it gave readers the choice of a different viewpoint. Unfortunately, that was not always the case in other parts of the region, where I was recommended not to travel to one country; and my business associations cut off as a result of my writings.

I persisted nonetheless strongly believing that it was time for the region to start thinking of new ways to govern its affairs. This belief would lead me to heavily research and travel throughout the region. The more I researched, the more confident I became of my conclusions—so much so that I soon decided to write a book about it. Inevitable Democracy in the Arab World: New Realities in an Ancient Land[2] would not be accepted at first by many publishers, and I received one rejection after another from trade as well as academic publishers. Considering the unfolding chaos in Iraq, no doubt they believed the book and its primary argument of democratic inevitability to be folly.

As I write this now, I confess that my personal satisfaction from having reached the correct conclusion pales next to the profound happiness I feel seeing the region finally take its destiny back into its own hands. Indeed my faith in the inevitability of democracy in the Arab world has only grown stronger by the day with lessons now being drawn from the smallest of Arab towns to the largest of cities.

But my personal journey writing about the Arab world started way before, with one Op Ed piece. It was titled: Arab Democracy—The Dream Scenario.

---

2 The first manuscript in 2005 had the book title, New Realities in an Old World: Inevitable Democracy in the Arab World. When it was published by Palgrave MacMillan in 2012, the name changed to Inevitable Democracy in the Arab World, New Realities in an Ancient Land.

Arab democracy—the dream scenario (April 2003)[3]

It may appear rather presumptuous to play out democracy's potential in the Middle East with war in Iraq only weeks old. But it is precisely because it is only beginning and so many doubts are already being cast that it is important to talk about how democracy is likely to pan out in the Arab world.

Before embarking on this exercise, there has to be some basic assumptions made. The primary assumption has to be that the US wins the war and Saddam Hussein and his regime are removed. The secondary assumption is that US intentions are not to pump and dump Iraq—rather to keep it intact with reconstruction in the same spirit of Germany and Japan after World War II. A tertiary assumption is that early US military control will eventually pave the way for long-term economic ties—although it is very likely that US military bases will be in Iraq for many decades to come as some still are in Europe and Japan.

With all these assumptions what are the chances of democracy proliferating in the Arab region? Unlike others, I believe the chances are quite strong; and this is how it could play out.

While Iraq is being institutionally democratized, the US is likely to press hard on the Israeli-Palestinian front to appease the Arab world.

Neither Americans, Israelis, nor the Palestinians will accept anything less than a democratic Palestine. With or without Arafat, there will be those who may fear the Islamic militants taking over. However, with a decisive and fair settlement, the very cause fueling the militants' support would have been diluted. Instead, the Palestinians tired of their predicament will likely vote for leaders who can lead them out of their economic misery.

Syria will follow. To some, this may come as a surprise prediction. However, in the context of an Israeli-Palestinian accord, the Syrians are unlikely to be left wanting on Israel's northern border. A quick resolution to the Golan question would lead to a peace between the Israelis and Syrians—not too distant from the almost-signed 90s deal.

The Syrian regime will hence see the hardline wind taken out of its sails. Of course, Syria is fortunate to have a young leader, who even though

---

3 First published in Lebanon's Daily Star on April 2, 2003.

brought in on the coat tails of his father's legacy, has already shown a desire for reform. With regional peace and democratic movements flanking Syria, even skeptics will see the futility in the old ways. Having thus delivered the peace and supported by his eager people, the young president will lead an orderly, gradual, and bloodless transformation to democracy.[4]

Of course, peace between Syria and Israel will automatically mean peace with Lebanon, whose foreign policy has been intertwined with that of Syria since the first Gulf War. Unlike that war, however, in which the Syrians supported and then held the Americans to their word requiring Lebanon to be under their geopolitical influence; this time around, their opposition of it will lead to Lebanese geopolitical independence. With Syria's influence sidelined, Lebanon's democracy will emerge—albeit sectarian.

Jordan—already close to the US—will also have no problems turning its absolute monarchy into a democratic one. It has a young king whose desire to reform has been hampered by regional tensions. With peace, those fears will have been eliminated. Jordan's push coupled with some other similar initiatives taking place in minor Gulf Cooperation States, such as Bahrain and Qatar, are bound to influence the rest of the Gulf, particularly the UAE, Kuwait, Oman, and Yemen.

Saudi Arabia will probably be the last in the Gulf to adopt a full democracy; and it will probably waiver in its efforts because of its insecurities and fears—ever so intertwined with its central Islamic position, its oil, as well as its complex royal structure.

However, if the US wisely leaves Saudi territory having secured bases in Iraq, and with most of the region democratizing, the kingdom will find it hard not to relinquish some of its power to its people. The thorny issue will be succession. Again, if Saudi Arabia is wise enough, it may see that democracy is in fact its way out of the succession problem, reducing it to a royal family affair rather than a national crisis.

Once they see their Levant and Gulf brethren moving toward democracy, North African nations are unlikely to hold out too long. With the US

---

4 In retrospect and as civil war currently rages on in Syria, this particular prediction seems pretty wishful.

pushing democracy in the other Arab regions, it will find it hard to continue to support the current Egyptian regime. The Algerians, Libyans, and Sudanese will probably wait, but it will be a matter of time.

Is this a naïve scenario? Recent history supports it happening much more so than anarchy or extremism. How many nations or regions today live in anarchy? How many developing regions including Latin America, South and East Asia, and the entire ex-Soviet Union are extreme in their orientation? If anything, most have been shifting to democracy.

Arabs are no different. They relish their dignity, their peace, and their freedom like everyone else. It may take several years, but my bet remains on the 300 million Arab voices. The price of Iraq's toil, blood, and sacrifice is so very high; but in the long term, it may very well lead our region to a more participatory future. We should never forget it; and rather try to make the most of it.

New realities in an old world (April 2003)[5]

In trying to understand the implications of the geopolitical developments in the Middle East, it is crucial to understand two factors: strategic geopolitical context and motive-guided interests. Only then can one draw possible scenarios and conclusions. Until now, many Arabs seem convinced that US motives are correlated with oil, Israel, or some neo-imperial ideology from the Christian right and fueled by lobby groups led by Jews and Texans. Not surprisingly, they have reached the direst of conclusions and are writing off any other scenarios that could emerge. But do these forgone conclusions pass the geopolitical context and interest tests?

Let's begin with oil. Oil is indeed a crucial lifeline for America's economy. However, can anyone claim that America did not already exercise strategic oil hegemony over the Middle East even before this war? All GCC countries continue to be among America's strongest allies, and have even supplied it with military bases. As for Iraqi oil, the US—through the UN—already had a stranglehold on Iraqi oil and could have maintained it for years to come.

---

5 First published in Lebanon's Daily Star on April 18, 2003.

With its regional oil interests already firmly placed, somehow the marginal benefit for America of directly rather than indirectly controlling Iraqi oil becomes dubious and doesn't quite pass the geopolitical-context test.

How about Israel? Some ask if it stands to benefit from an Iraq free of Saddam. This, however, is not the right question. The right one is: Was America ready to place such an unprecedented bet simply to please Israel and a diluted Jewish American lobby? (Up until the beginning of the war, polls showed that a large portion of American Jews were actually against the war.)

Even though in the past America has gone out of its way to please Israel, it is difficult to believe that even the staunchest of Bush administration hawks would risk their relationships with NATO, the UN, Europe and Russia—not to mention America's economic and soft-power (ideological power), simply to please Israel.

They could have done so simply by continuing to turn the other way from all of Israel's atrocities in the Palestinian territories and calling Sharon "a man of peace". The fact that the US announced a "road map" and with Blair insisting on placing it on the coalition's top of the post-war Iraq list—not to mention Sharon's recent declaration of giving up settlements for peace—further refute the claim.

As for American imperialist intentions, it passed neither the geopolitical-context test nor the interest's one. Why would the US go to the Middle East, of all places, to spearhead its imperial ambitions? Surely it can find better targets. South America, for instance, would be logistically much simpler and is a region geographically and ideologically closer, several times richer, and more productive than the Arab world.

These are but a few examples of claims of America's motives and intentions crisscrossing our region. Of course, they all lead to pumping (oil) and dumping (regimes) scenarios. Adding fuel to this mix is tragic Iraqi casualties, wounded Arab pride, and the ever-present usage of Islam—a religion tragically battered and bruised by anyone with political or military interests in our region.

But if the above American intentions are not true, what is it then, and from which geopolitical context is it being drawn? The primary geopolitical context governing American policies since September 11, 2001 is September 11. Any other context may be complementary, but it remains subsidiary.

What does this mean? Quite simply, September 11 awoke America to the realization that the Middle East is politically dysfunctional. Of course this was not news. What changed with September 11, however, was that these growing dysfunctions came back to haunt America on its own soil. Therefore, what many claim is American bullying is quite the opposite; by implicitly uprooting Saddam, America has also uprooted its own previous bankrupt policies in the region.

Therefore, America's interests, unlike what many regional skeptics claim, may indeed have changed to be aligned with those of the Arab people—that is, if our people believe democracy, freedom, and capitalism are things that are also in their interests.

With this in mind, a different set of possibilities emerges. For one, Iraq would not be pumped and dumped, but rather supported by the US and given what it needs to become truly democratic. By Iraq becoming another Arab ally, America, from its own perspective, avoids it being a terrorist breeding ground, a weapon of mass destruction threat, a regional instability factor, and yes, it also benefits from a reliable oil supply. Also, by being in Iraq, America can now withdraw its forces from Saudi Arabia, further avoiding any contentious calamities with militant Islam and a repeat of September 11.

Paralleling all this would be the Israeli-Palestinian peace. With American and European (Blair) brokerage, if Palestine finally emerges, it also benefits America in gaining popular Arab support, in supporting a secure Israel, and in dampening Islamic militants' usage of Palestine as a battle cry. To top it off, if the above eventually dominoes democracy into the region, then all the better.

Is the above not in the interest of America and the Arabs simultaneously? If it is in the interest of both, my sincere hope is that my fellow Arabs do not let their old world pains and pride stand in the way of new realities, which through some convoluted divinity may have finally brought America's long-term interests with those of our people and region. It is also my hope that when the peace going gets tough, America does not shirk or lose sight of why it went there.

Democracy 101—Lessons from Lebanon (April 2003)[6]

In light of Iraq's support of pre- and post-independence Lebanon, it is only fair in its hour of need that Lebanon reciprocates. As the Lebanese treasury seems to be in as serious a calamity as some Baghdad banks, sending money may not be an option. But there may be something much more valuable Lebanon can offer: democratic experience. It is commonly accepted that the only Arab country with any steady constitutional democracy has been Lebanon. While some may dispute this very point, their argument is incorrect in that it is absolute. In other words, the fact that democracy in Lebanon is not perfect does not mean it does not exist. With this caveat, and for whatever it's worth, here are some valuable lessons from Lebanon's democracy that I hope would benefit Iraq.

Lebanon is a parliamentary democracy. This means that the people's power is channeled through a parliament. This legislative body is elected every four years. Voters cast ballots in the districts in which they are registered, and they can vote for individual candidates or lists running for office. As Lebanon has a kaleidoscopic variety of sects and religions, parliament was designed with a rigid sectarian representation that guarantees representation to all. Once in office, parliament "votes" for the president, prime minister, and speaker—each of whom also has to be of a particular sect.

On the bright side, Lebanon's democracy has managed to survive six decades. In a region as treacherous as that of the Middle East, it seems nothing short of amazing that Lebanon has never seen a coup d'état. Notwithstanding two presidential assassinations, Lebanon has consistently transferred executive power between unrelated politicians (in today's Arab world, this is no small accomplishment). In the only few cases where consecutive executives were related, their election seems to have been more an emotional reaction to assassination than to autocratic ambitions. All the while, Lebanon has been privileged to enjoy a relatively free press, a capitalist system and a vibrant society.

Unfortunately, the above does not paint the whole picture, and Lebanon's democracy could not circumvent several civil crises, culminating

---

6   First published in Lebanon's Daily Star on April 25, 2003.

in a catastrophic civil war. Adding insult to injury, most of the surrounding autocratic regimes did not fail. While this seems counterintuitive—and rather unfair given Lebanon's pioneering democratic efforts—it should be made clear that Lebanon's state did not fail because of democracy, but because of a lousy democratic design. It is here where important lessons can be drawn from Lebanon's experience.

In designing their democracy, the ever-enterprising Lebanese attempted an impossible trinity: rigid parliamentary representation, institutionalized conflict in the executive branch, and a weak state. In terms of the first, politicians consistently failed to create a malleable political system capable of adapting to changing realities within the social and economic structure—socioeconomic disparities were among the primary reasons behind the civil war.

In terms of executive conflict, because of the institutionalized sectarian structure, a leader is eternally split between representing the nation (which is the responsible thing) and representing the sect (which is the politically rational thing). As no cross-sectarian political parties have been able to emerge, it becomes a no-brainer for the leader to fall back on his sect to keep a support base. Unfortunately, as each of the executives comes from a different sect, the political battles typically occur along sectarian lines; worse yet, they do not occur during elections, but during rule.

As for the weak state—as if all these sectarian checks and balances had not been enough—politicians have consistently rejected any efforts to have a strong state apparatus that inhibits disintegration.

This failure in design was not due to a lack of insight on the part of the Lebanese forefathers. On the contrary, contemporaries warned of the impending clash between sectarian and national interests—so much so, that these warnings were integrated into the constitution advising eventual amendment when "circumstances permitted."

Essentially, unable to muster enough clout to make such fundamental political building-block compromises, Lebanese forefathers pushed the dilemma unto their sons, who once again in 1989 pushed it unto theirs. But blaming the forefathers for political sectarianism is not fair—it had been there for centuries. Where they did fail was in over-emphasizing the sectarian structure in government—when they could have compromised by institutionalizing it in parliament, but kept the executive positions as a free-of-sectarianism vent for healthy competition and direct national election by all Lebanese.

So, my Iraqi friends, while you labor to find your democratic path, have faith, use your common sense, be inquisitive, and do not be afraid of the unknown. Democracy is by its very definition for everyone, so do not be cheated by those claiming superior legitimacy or knowledge. You will face very daunting dilemmas; be patient and patriotic. Whatever you do, try not to stitch your democracy only along sectarian seams; for in the long term, political crises will end up splitting it along those same seams as it has repeatedly done in Lebanon.

Arab intelligentsia walks a tightrope (May 2003)

Arab intelligentsia, carpe diem! In the run-up to the Iraq war, much of the Arab intelligentsia walked a tightrope. While not wanting to be perceived as supporting Saddam Hussein's Baathist regime, they vigorously condemned America for wanting to get rid of him. Even before the first bullet had been fired, Arab intelligentsia typewriters banged away in New York, London, and Paris finding America guilty of warmongering, oil robbing, and colonization.

What is ironic is that the intelligentsia is by definition enlightened and hence liberal in its inclination. Recently though, the Arab intelligentsia accidentally found itself in the unorthodox position of defending one of the most repressive regimes in the world against one of the most liberal. How did that twist of fate come about? There were several reasons. With the war over, it is important to understand them, for they will affect the development of some of the liberal ideas being propagated.

The first reason for this twist is chronic disenchantment. Arabs over the past several decades have become disillusioned with lack of economic opportunity, political representation, and social stability. Pan-Arabism failed. Autocracies failed. Military dictatorships failed. Being at the forefront of some of these movements, it is not surprising that the Arab intelligentsia has turned skeptical. The key questions to be asked here are therefore: Has the intelligentsia become so disenchanted that it will give up at the moment when real liberal reform may finally be emerging? Will they no longer preach for the one social ideal that has yet to be tried in their region—democracy—because it was forcefully brought in by America, even if it is closest to their principles?

This brings us to the second reason: Arab pride. After centuries of military defeat and humiliation by external powers, some Arabs perceive their pride to be all that remains and obstinately take counterintuitive positions even ones in apparent self-disinterest—Palestinian suicide bombings of Israeli civilians as opposed to Israeli military targets being a case in point. While pride is good, unbridled pride risks blindness and perhaps even ridicule, such as met the declarations of Mohammed Saeed Al Sahhaf, the Iraqi information minister, still claiming victory on television as American tanks could be seen rolling in the background. For this to occur within a very closed and isolated Baathist Iraq may be understandable; however, for it to also occur to Arab thinkers living in much less repressive environments with access to information and news points to a more serious problem. There comes a time when humility, national interest and the desire to learn from mistakes must be made more expedient than pride. Germany and Japan after World War II are good examples to learn from, having risen from humiliation by sheer hard work, intelligence; and yes, why not, a bit of national pride.

The third reason for the Arab intelligentsia's misalignment was its misunderstanding of the Arab street. While it may be easy to blame the intelligentsia, in reality does anyone in the Arab world truly know what the Arab street wants? Everybody was saying that Iraqis loved Saddam Hussein until the images of them trampling on his fallen statue's head emerged. While some may point to polls, what is it exactly that these polls are measured against when little if any institutionalized opposition exists to come up with alternative ideas; when political process for the most part is imaginary, generating chronic apathy; and when clientelism reigns supreme? Could it be that all the Arab street wants is practical solutions—freedom to think and work, perhaps?

The fourth reason is simply geopolitical miscalculation. Pre-September 11, 2001 Cold War intrigue was over utilized, post-September 11, 2001 realities ignored, American intentions and interests misunderstood, and Iraqi power and regime allegiance overestimated. Nevertheless, it was surprising to see some renowned expatriate Arab thinkers sticking to over-simplistic and outdated conspiracy theories when indications pointed to fundamental shifts in US policy towards Iraq and the region in general.

With all this said, what does it all mean to the future of the region? Essentially, it means one of two scenarios. One is that the Arab intelligentsia puts the past behind it, Arab pride aside, and searches for a flicker within itself to light a torch that carries a liberal democratic message. Another scenario is that it could bury itself under a heap of past disappointments, emerging only to regain what little pride it perceives still remains through futile and unconstructive attacks on any reform initiative coming to the region.

Recently, many typewriters have fallen silent. My hope is that this is a sign of introspection and not surrender, because a difference can yet be made. Arab intelligentsia, carpe diem!

"City Yes, Ali No"—State, religion and US forces in Iraq (May 2003)[7]

"City yes, Ali no," the massive Iraqi crowds in the city of Najaf shouted emotionally at the advancing US forces. They were trying to get the message across to the American soldiers that they were free to enter the city itself; but not the city's holy shrine where Ali, the prophet's son-in-law, was laid to rest many centuries ago. After some minor mix-ups, the Americans listened, retreated—some even bowing in the process—and bypassed the shrine. They took control of Najaf shortly afterward with little resistance.

As previously oppressed Iraqis begin to enjoy their newly gained freedoms, the US and the rest of the world are trying to decipher the dichotomy and dynamics between religion and state within Iraq.

---

7 First published in the Daily Star on May 3, 2003.

Underlying this concern is whether or not the Shiites in Iraq will try to Islamize Iraq and hence cause "collateral" damage to the US's democratization plans? To the Americans, the Shiite organized masses have come as a surprise—at least the "organized" part. The US policy options are not easy—as Patrick Seale pointed out recently. On the one hand, if the Americans do nothing, they fear it will come back and bite them as it did in Iran. On the other hand, if they do something to quell these masses, it will create resentment and confirm what many in Iraq already feel is an occupation. Of course, another option is picking up their US Army duffel bags and bidding Iraq good-bye. As much as many in the world may wish it, this is out of the question at this point.

So, what is it America can do? Quite simply, listen to the Najaf crowds by avoiding "Ali" and focusing instead on the "city." Of all people, the Americans are the best positioned to do so. They have the deepest tradition when it comes to the separation of—and coexistence between—religion and state. While some may argue that the neo-conservative Christian right is in itself a refutation of such a separation, claiming that the neo-cons wield disproportionate political power at this juncture in American political history is one thing, and claiming that they now control all of the US's political and state affairs and may change its fundamental political constitution is a completely different thing. Few, if anyone, can seriously claim the latter with any convincing arguments.

By concentrating on the "city" (economics, the environment, health, infrastructure, security etc.), the Americans stand to benefit in many ways.

For one, it comes naturally to them. They understand it and are likely to be more successful deploying it. Second, they can show that they are not in Iraq with any religious agenda, but with a civil mission to restore order and lead Iraq to a democratic path. Third, the Americans avoid falling into the trap of taking sides. Even being perceived to be doing so is dangerous enough. Fourth, by focusing on the "city," the Americans essentially maintain strategic initiative. If, however, they fall into murky religious issues, they risk losing strategic initiative and getting bogged down in a vicious cycle fueled by internal and external forces eager to see America fall flat on its face.

But what about "Ali?" Surely with today's 24/7 global news frenzy, America can't simply ignore it. How should America deal with the religious fervor and its potential effects on Iraq's emerging polity? While understanding and respecting local religious and political nuances is important, the US should be careful to keep their eye on what they said they wanted to do in the first place: help establish a true Iraqi democracy. But what does this really mean in practical terms? It means the US goal should not be to help pick a winning politician or religious group, but rather to help pick a winning democratic process or formula acceptable to all Iraqi groups.

Once this is done, all the Americans need to do is make sure whoever comes to power does nothing to change the pre-agreed-to rules of the new democratic game (i.e. the emerging Iraqi constitution). America should avoid at all costs getting implicated in any political meddling mess because it would trigger a vicious cycle by bolstering fundamentalist claims. If Islamists win elections, America should respect it as long as they do not then trample on the rights of others. More importantly, the US should guarantee that subsequent elections allow participation.

For anyone still doubting the democratic potential of the common Arab layman, what better rebuttal than the chanting crowds in Najaf who even under such adverse conditions still came out on the streets demanding their clear desire not to mix "city" and "Ali." Fortunately, the Americans listened... and hopefully they will continue to do so.

Pacing change or changing pace? (May 2003)[8]

As Arab regimes begin to feel the heat from masses wanting change—as well as the international community tired of popular repression whip-lashing into their own backyards—an interesting theme that has come to the fore is the pace in which change should occur—change meaning reform. While one typically finds that regimes in the Arab world do not always agree with change; if and when they finally get around to it, they resort to the paternalistic argument of it needing to be done at a slow pace so as not to

---

8   First published in Lebanon's Daily Star on May 26, 2003.

negatively affect the dynamics of the region. Anything rash, they warn, would yield "undesired results" pointing to revolutionary Iran, Algeria's civil war, Afghanistan's Taliban, and the Islamic militants supposedly waiting in the shadows in Palestine, Lebanon and Saudi Arabia.

But if one thinks about it, will the problems be solved by pacing change or rather by changing pace? Is our region's predicament due to the speed of reforms that have been introduced, or is it due to slow or never-seriously-introduced-in-the-first-place reforms? Since the Arab world itself does not offer much experience on reform, one needs to look to other places. Unfortunately, history does not seem to be consistent with respect to the pace of reform. Sometimes a quick split with the past has yielded reasonably good results, as was the case with the 18th century American Revolution, the 19th century Japanese Meiji Restoration, and the 20th century end of the Soviet Union. Sometimes slow change has also worked, such as the case of modern China and, to a certain degree, Chile and Spain.

Closer to home, ironically, many of the regimes now calling for slow change themselves came to power through very quick and revolutionary upheaval. Indeed, Arab history reached its zenith in the previous millennium on the heels of a blitzkrieg conquest—seldom seen before or since. So, where exactly does this notion of the requirement for so slow a pace of change in the Arab world come from—particularly when economic and socio political theories do not give clear guidance? Could it be self-interest? Is it not evident that self-interest exists with anyone who has been in power for decades—or has benefited from it—to call for unhurried change?

Then again, could it not be genuine fear? Autocratic Arab regimes may have much to fear for their murky past and their opaque policies. Would those who are socio-economically distraught react violently, would families of abducted loved ones take revenge, or would religious zealots take over? While all these fears may be legitimate, an equally legitimate question is why the ruling regimes have not been able to circumvent them. Surely, "insufficient time" could not have been a factor, as most of these regimes have been in power for decades.

While Rome was not built in a day, much less-endowed contemporary—and yet equally complex—societies (such as Japan, Korea, Taiwan, and Singapore) all reformed and as a result have become much freer.

What is it that Arab regimes can do going forward? For one, they can continue to do nothing. Regimes have been in power for decades. But they would do this at their own peril—as Saddam Hussein saw firsthand, and as the Saudis and Palestinians are seeing now with all the turmoil around them. A second option is for them to simply pack up and leave—a risky proposition, and perhaps not the optimal one, as economic strife and religious fervor could lead to regional anarchy. The third option is to genuinely speed up political, economic, social and educational reform. Risky? Of course it is, but not more than the risks of doing nothing or pacing reform at a snail's pace.

At a time when the region is going through some tough times, it can still count its blessings for the resource endowment that God has bequeathed it. However, it must also use it for the benefit of improving the well-being of the people.

Ceding more power to the people should also take center stage. What the region needs most now is a fraternal changing of the pace of reform as opposed to a paternal pacing of change. This should not be done by feeding them, but by trusting them and making them responsible for their own decisions and lives.

Lebanese jaw-jaw is better than Iraqi war-war (June 2003)[9]

Around 1993, both Iraq and Lebanon were coming out of two different wars. While Iraq was trying to charter its way out of its first Gulf War fiasco, Lebanon was trying to draw a future out of a devastating 15-year civil war.

Ten years later, Lebanon is back on its feet. Unfortunately, Iraq fell into an abyss. Surely, few in the world would have guessed it back then. After all, Iraq had a typical governing Arab regime and Lebanon didn't. Iraq had

---

9 First published in Lebanon's Daily Star on June 14, 2003.

an autocrat leading one regime for decades; no political representation; lots of oil to grease the economy; and a relatively docile population led by a minority. Ironically, Lebanon had to cope with a kaleidoscope of conflicting opinions, visions, and affiliations. What sense can we make of this? What lessons can be drawn for Iraq in 2003?

Back in 1993, Lebanon's internal destruction was much more comprehensive than that of Iraq. Lebanon had to cope with a completely destroyed, inadequate, and obsolete infrastructure, with few if any fully standing governmental institutions, no political parties—at the time most were militias that had just been disbanded. The Lebanese Army emerging from the war was ineffective and needed revamping. The country was still occupied, with resistance activities still being carried out. The economy was in shambles with endemic inflation. Uncertainty kept long-term investors out and short-term speculators in. Society itself was still in a post-war shell shock. Skepticism and pessimism reigned supreme. Anyone with half a chance to leave did.

Iraq of 1993, however, did not have to cope with as much overall destruction. From a military perspective its forces were still intact as was proven in the subsequent quelling of Shiite uprisings shortly after the allies had departed. While the economy was indeed on the brink, Iraq's massive oil reserves were still very much intact. Its governmental institutions were in control and so was the reigning Baath Party. Society itself did not have to undergo the pain of a prolonged civil war—the entire Gulf War had lasted a mere few months. So at the time, arguably Iraq's society could not have been as traumatized as the Lebanese one.

And yet while all predictions may have pointed to the contrary, by 2003 Lebanon had fared much better than Iraq. Why? Quite simply, the Lebanese political system for all its impervious deficiencies allowed for dialogue. While there have been some black spots, few can argue that over the past ten years there has not been all sorts of dialogue from diverse Lebanese regions, social classes, religions, ages, and backgrounds.

This dialogue may not have been orderly or pretty; and yet a dialogue galore it was—so much so that Finance Minister Fouad Sinyora once joked he may start taxing it—and it helped Lebanon rehabilitate itself internally and reintegrate with the world community. Lebanon in 2003 is a different country from that of 1993—granted there remain serious issues to be dealt with.

Through its relatively open dialogue, Lebanon's perceived weakness—the diversity of its people and opinions—proved to be still stronger and persevering than what at one point was being termed as the most powerful armed autocracy in the region. Proponents for limiting dialogue in its many forms should always remember this.

Unfortunately, autocratic conditions in Iraq did not allow except for a single-tracked dialogue. Internally, its people—diverse as they are—found themselves forcibly marching to the uniform beat of a single man's obstinate regime never able to entertain other what-ifs or how-abouts. Externally, it is ludicrous to even think now that Iraqi dialogue was being presented to the world by the likes of ex-Information Minister Mohammed Saeed Al Sahhaf.

This deficiency alienated Iraq from its neighbors and the world—so much so that the UN imposed an embargo on the entire nation for a decade. Iraqis found themselves heading toward a precipice. One indelibly has to wonder had the Iraqi system wisely allowed for a more inclusive dialogue—even one as wobbly as Lebanon's—what choices would have been available to Iraq and to the international community. Instead Saddam Hussein maintained his 100 percent voting record and allowed no other voice or opinion to emerge. If Lebanon's post-war experience is of any value, even the powerful and wealthy Prime Minister Rafic Hariri was self-admittedly "sent home" in 1998, and had to work hard to get back his premiership job in 2000.

How does all this affect Iraq in 2003? Iraqis should rejoice. If the Americans have brought anything with them to Iraq, it is an insatiable capacity to accept multilateral dialogue (political, journalistic...). It is the bedrock of American society, and one which they arguably value the most next to freedom.

The good news is that all signs have so far shown that there is already public dialogue. And if someone is still unsure about its potential positive effects, the question to ask is, "Have you been to Lebanon lately?"

The fallacy of Iraq's war justifications (July 2003)[10]

In the Arab region these days, one hears all kinds of arguments for the US invasion of Iraq including the oil argument, the colonial empire argument, the naiveté argument, not to mention the ludicrous family vendetta argument (Bush versus Hussein). Let us look at some of these in greater detail.

The oil argument goes something like this: America needs to guarantee its global supply of oil and is willing to go to great lengths to achieve it—even the invasion of a sovereign country. This argument is at best frail because the US has actually lost oil supplies in many other parts of the world, but has not gone to war over them. In the Gulf, the US already had enough bases in Saudi Arabia, Kuwait, Bahrain, and Qatar. Its control of Persian Gulf Oil since the first Iraqi War is undisputed. In fact, if anything, keeping Saddam in place would have been an even further excuse to maintain—if not strengthen—its military presence and hold over the region. In such a case, the US could have presented to the United Nations—and much more easily have gotten—a resolution for simply a stricter embargo on Iraq, keeping Hussein in place and all its Gulf bases intact. Would this not have tightened its hold on regional Gulf oil even further? The answer is, yes, very likely. The only problem with this argument—and which the US administration knows very well—is that it would not have helped in its war against global terrorism. On the contrary, it would have fueled even more Arab resentment leading perhaps to further attacks such as 9/11. So what actually happened was not only did the US decide to go to war in Iraq to unseat Hussein, but soon afterwards—and rather quietly—it withdrew from most of its Saudi bases. Surely, the US had not forgotten its oil interests in Saudi Arabia? No, it hadn't; but it had not forgotten the calamity of September 11th either and it is beginning to work both the military side (war in Iraq) and the softer democratic tracks (call for regional reform).

As for the colonial empire argument, history has shown that the United States as a nation has indeed become a global empire that influences the affairs of the world. And yet paradoxically its people and ideology harbor as much colonial ambitions as they do a monarchy. The actions of the United

---

10 First published in Lebanon's Daily Star on July 3, 2003.

States after the end of World War II is proof positive of this simple fact. While the United States occupied nations such as Italy, France, Germany, and Japan, one would be hard pressed to argue that they had colonial ambitions in these occupations. After all, they did not limit the trade of these nations, they did not limit their interaction with other states, and they did not impose cultural beliefs—with the exception of democracy and capitalism—both of which are not really patented products of the United States anyway. In all cases, while the US maintained some form of military presence, by no means was it akin to British or French behavior or control in their Indian or North African colonies, respectively. Nor was it similar to the Soviet Union, which at its apex after World War II also seems to have come much closer to a formal form of colonialism by turning countries such as East Germany, Czechoslovakia, Poland, Hungary, and the Baltics into satellite states, whose entire government structure, military, police, education, economies, planning, and products followed strict Soviet guidelines.

Some may still argue, that even though the US has not harbored it in the past, it does not mean that it does not have intentions of being a colonial empire in the future. Harvard's Joseph Nye argues to the contrary, stating that American power in the second half of the 20th Century did not come only from the deployment of hard (military or economic) power, but also from soft power, which in its simplest form, he defines as "getting others to want what you want." Soft power is what allowed Western Europe to maintain a stronger grip on their freedoms as provided for by democracy and capitalism, vis-à-vis the Soviet satellite states, which overtime grew tired of Soviet stifling. Projecting this forward, Dr. Nye argues that,

"Power in the twenty-first century will rest on a mix of hard and soft resources. No country is better endowed than the United States in all three dimensions—military, economic, and soft power. Our greatest mistake in such a world would be to fall into one-dimensional analysis and to believe that investing in military power will ensure our strength."

A concern for such a balance would hardly be the aspiration of a colonial power. For the US to shift all of a sudden into a neo-colonial power following in the footsteps of Sixteenth century Spain in Latin America, Nineteenth Century Britain in South Asia, or Twentieth century France in North Africa seems far-fetched. For it to decide at the beginning of the 21st century to colonize a rather hostile and under-developed Arab world, which the US realizes is so culturally different and complex, seems even more ludicrous and a hard argument to sell to an objective observer.

As for the naiveté argument, there is some notion that Europeans are more sophisticated in international affairs than the United States; and that democracy in the Arab world cannot be introduced or imposed in the manner it is being done in Iraq. European colonial history spanning more than six centuries is cited as proof; and it is said that unlike the United States' predominantly isolated history, European global adventurism has lent it to being more culturally nuanced and sensitive in global geopolitics.

This claim in itself is ridiculously generalist in its "European" definition; as the British, Spanish, Italian, Portuguese and Polish all actually supported US actions in Iraq with ground troops. So the first question it begs is how "European" is Europe? Are any of these less "European" than the French and Germans who opposed the invasion? But even were one to take the argument at face value, is it not just as hard to argue for European geopolitical "maturity" when a mere decade ago Europe had not been able to stop the barbarous Yugoslavian war in its own back yard without US intervention? The British themselves—arguably the most experienced of Europeans in international affairs—were not able to resolve the Irish question without the intervention of the United States either. And if "maturity" and "sophistication" be the primary measuring stick in global affairs, how could those opposing introducing democracy by force justify supporting taking it away by force? Was this not the tragic case in Algeria in 1991, when France was the main supporter (or as some would have it non-opposer) of the military junta's coup ousting the Algerian President and his democratically elected parliament, simply because they were Islamists? Of course, they argue that Algerian Islamic "reform" was a mere front for an Islamic theocracy, similar to that of Iran's. But if that were the case, and if the military was there to intervene, why not wait until *after* the Islamists actually committed the 'democratic crime' of usurping power, before dooming the country's democratic election results and delving the nation into a vicious decade old war? Is this the sort of geopolitical "maturity" that the Arab region needs?

Mired in its endless web of calamities, the last thing the Arab region needs is a good-cop bad-cop routine by Western powers, who at the end of the day are all looking for their own interests—as France did to its interests in Algeria, the US is doing in Iraq and the Arab world; and as indeed the Arabs themselves must learn to do within an increasingly complex world. In the case of the US, its post 9/11 interests seem to have finally aligned with potentially emerging Arab democracies. If this is characterized as American naiveté, then so be it—although it does beg the question as to whether or not it was this very same naïveté that saved geopolitically "mature" Europe from its self-destruction a mere six decades ago.

And finally for the rather humorous Bush-Hussein vendetta theory, it is too ludicrous to even consider, unless of course one is willing to believe the Bush family exerts such power that not only is it able to manipulate the entire American system, but that of Britain, Australia, Poland, Italy, Spain, and countless others in the UN in an incredibly massive conspiracy.

On liberalizing and democratizing the Arab world (January 2004)

It is important to differentiate between liberalization and democratization. The first is typically more on the economic and perhaps to a certain degree on the social side of things. Whereas democratization is typically more on the political side of things. Generally speaking, liberalization can occur with or without democratization. In the Arab world, it can happen under autocracy or oligarchy (Qatar, UAE), dictatorship (Libya), or single party regimes (Egypt under Mubarak). All tried liberalizing their economies. None were democratized. The opposite rarely holds true; and democratization almost always ushers in liberalization—otherwise the whole enterprise turns into a plutocracy of sorts.

When it comes to liberalization, it typically uncovers many hidden economic truths kept away by the autocratic regimes from more than just democratization. In fact, societies that manage to liberalize and bear the brunt before democracy is introduced (for example Chile), tend to feel less the effects once democracy does actually emerge. In the region, one would expect a country like the UAE, which has been liberalizing for almost two decades, to fair much better say than Libya, which is just beginning to liberalize.

Democratization without liberalization is unusual and can be considered a paradox of sorts. Walking through Soweto's Apartheid museum leaves a visitor wondering how South Africa could have considered itself democratic during the apartheid era, when a vast portion of its black population did not enjoy the same rights as their white South African counterparts. The same in the United States in the pre-civil rights and universal suffrage eras. Latin America in the 1980's saw its dictatorships fall by the wayside before its economies had had a chance to liberalize—namely Colombia, but this quickly proved to be an untenable situation and the economy was quickly liberalized under the banner of "El Nuevo Liberalismo" or the New Liberalism.

True liberalization and democratization in the long run need to go hand in hand because the premise of a true democracy is to allow people to make their own political, economic, and social choices within the confines of the law of the land. In other words, ultimately democracy allows the masses to institutionally decide what is or is not in their best interests. To get to that point without an accompanying liberalization is a rather futile exercise. Similarly, liberalization without an emerging democracy in most cases (except perhaps in the wealth abundant trucial Gulf States) will prove to be untenable.

This said, one should not be under the impression that liberalized democracies will bloom overnight in the Arab World. It will take many of these nations at least a generation to consolidate emerging democracies—during which time they are likely to face increasing socio-economic pressure—primarily explosive demographic growth. But the region has also been endowed with resources, which can be deployed to its own development and the successful emergence of truly liberalized democracies.

Top-down versus bottom-up economics (February 2004)

"With no growth, maintaining per student expenditure in education in Jordan would require a doubling of education's budget share of total spending over the decade…. Sharing costs with the private sector and donors can ease the burden on public finances[11]".

The key to the above expert is the "sharing of costs". In the Jordanian example, with a ballooning population, the government is finding it exceedingly hard to fully subsidize education. Therefore, "sharing of costs" can translate into two options: Either taxing the private sector to fund education or privatizing the schools and having the people pay for it directly. In either case, the cash-strapped government is essentially asking society to "share the costs". And while it may force some of it through autocratic means, it will have to negotiate with society one way or the other. For instance, while an Arab government can force the private sector to pay an education tax; unless it liberalized its policies that are holding back growth, it cannot force this same private sector to hire the droves of graduates. Of course, being cash-strapped means that it cannot hire them either, which leads to unemployment and social tensions. Similarly, the government cannot force the private sector to buy-up the assets if it chooses to begin an education privatization process, unless it can show that society can actually afford to pay for it. Again, if the economy is stagnant because of stifling conditions, it will not be able to impose an autocratic solution either. Hence, governments in the Arab world are slowly realizing that they need to negotiate with their societies through both political and economic liberalization—but more on this later on in the chapter.

It is therefore no surprise that in the Jordanian case, King Abdullah II has also been very eager to liberalize and privatize the economy as indicated by the implementation of the Free Trade Agreement signed with the US several years prior, and the opening of several QIZ's (free trade zones), or the privatization of the telecom industry. This, in turn, has led to a hike in

---

11   The World Bank, *Claiming the Future*, the World Bank, 1995, pg. 79.

investment not just from Jordanians, but also foreigners as far away as China wanting to take advantage of this newly liberalized economic environment. All this is bound to have positive repercussions on employment, as well as overall economic growth in Jordan going forward. Equally interesting has been the King's parallel willingness to include a sizeable contingent of Palestinian ministers in his cabinet—Palestinians, of course, are a very large constituent in Jordan, that had theretofore been kept outside of the royal courts.

Other Arab governments are finding it just as hard to cope with some of their economic calamity, while maintaining a stifling political grip. They are realizing that there is a compelling need to include other portions of society, particularly the private sector, into the decision-making process. This is bound to create its own dynamic, for if the private sector were made part of the process in which difficult policy decisions are understood and made; then it could pave the way for the proper sharing of economic responsibility. A striking case of shortcomings being faced by incumbent Arab regimes—which are forcing them to "negotiate" with other sectors in the economy and relinquish some political power—is that of Lebanon during the late 1990s.

Towards the late 1990's, fully realizing the economic calamity that could ensue if it defaulted on its US$30 billion in loans, the Lebanese government found itself needing to negotiate with different internal sectors of the economy (as well as external ones). In particular, it managed to negotiate with the privately held banking sector in Lebanon for an alleviation of some of its hefty interest burden. In close coordination with the Lebanese Central Bank, the Lebanese banks scooped up zero interest government bonds that replaced higher interest ones, thus "sharing costs" and saving hundreds of millions of interest payments.

Similarly and in trying to solve the same underlying economic problem, the government found itself needing to negotiate with the unions of stale State-Owned Enterprises (SOE's) such as the Lebanese national airlines, Middle East Airlines (MEA) so as to stop the financial hemorrhage. What used to be a lucrative private airline business serving the Middle East before the Lebanese civil war, had been left in shambles, and with an over-bloated unionized staff of some 3,000 working to operate less than a dozen planes. Facing bankruptcy, MEA was picked up by Lebanon's Central Bank, and infused with cash. This was not enough, however, and the airline continued to bleed because of its hefty but unproductive labor force. Many solutions were floated including shutting down operations, spin-off at fire sale pricing, and protective measures against competition. None took off, and an ineffective government was thrown out of office in 2000, in an unprecedented and peaceful democratic parliamentary election.

The new government, whose election mantra was execution, immediately began implementing a plan to retire many of the employees and revive the company. Negotiations with labor were difficult; but armed with a popular mandate to manage the sorry state of the economy, the elected government was able to sail through Lebanon's complex political web, retire thousands with "cost-sharing" measures, and in less than three years turn profitable MEA's operation—all at a time of a massive glut in the global airline industry, and an economically counter-intuitive Lebanese Open Skies policy that saw all kinds of airlines use landing rights at MEA's hub, Beirut International Airport.

Lebanon's economic problems have not been fully solved; and yet its democracy—as precarious as it may seem—has allowed it to have an open dialogue with different sectors of the economy in a way, which has helped it inch along. So far as the brief Lebanese cases have shown, everyone is pitching in—the government, the private sector, but credit also has to go to the Lebanese society as well. In 2002, for instance, a newly introduced value-added tax proved to be a resounding success.

While the Lebanese may grumble at paying this or that other tax, the fact remains that most have come to realize that considering the burgeoning national debt, it is inevitable. But this has also meant more and more, they are holding the government accountable. On a recent trip to Lebanon and one which happened to occur while the 2003-2004 budget was being debated in parliament, I remember watching the minister of finance appear on several talk shows to "sell" the budget. On one show, I recall him being drilled down to as much detail as a line item by the talk show host. Back in parliament, it was being reported that the debate was fiery with some 40 of the 128 parliamentarians demanding the floor[12]. Labor unions and teacher associations were just as boisterous. The budget would eventually pass, but not until after some adjustments that took some of society's demands into account—particularly on issues concerning school teachers and hospitals.

Criticism and accountability is coming from non-governmental quarters as well. Recently, an association of Lebanese property owners criticized a draft law that they perceived was preferential to lessees (of whom the government itself is the largest). They demanded that the Lebanese President "abide by his swearing-in speech"[13] to curb such forms of corruption and favoritism. All are but indications of the negotiations occurring between the Lebanese government and its society.

Going forward, the more the government will require its society's help, the more it will have to liberalize and accept being further scrutinized. More advanced nations seem to have reached this conclusion. Hopefully Arabs will too sooner rather than later.

On rebuilding Iraq—between massive & passive support (March 2004)

With the destruction being witnessed in Iraq, many in the Arab World are asking whether there will be a Marshall Plan to follow. Of course the Marshall Plan refers to the American plan reconstructing Western Europe at the end of World War II.

Notwithstanding Europe's urgent need, as the likes of Hogan have written, pushing through the Marshall Plan was by no means easy or smooth. Britain was against some of its tenets—primarily a unified Europe menacing its shores—for centuries it had been Britain's policy to maintain the division of Europe and thus keep it across the channel. Continental Europeans

---

12 "Parliament begins Fiery Budget Debate", *Naharnet*, January 23, 2003, Cited on January 07, 2004 from: http://www.naharnet.com/domino/tn/NewsDesk.nsf/0/28D4 C8AFDFD8BCFB42256CB6003B243C?OpenDocument&PRINT.

13 Arzouminian, Ara "Landlords take umbrage at new draft law on rents", *The Dailystar*, January 9, 2004, Cited on January 10, 2004 from http://www.dailystar.com. lb/business/09_01_04_d.asp

needed some convincing as well. It is still difficult to imagine how the French and Germans could even face one another, after so many years of war, let alone work with one another. Also, within the United States, there was no consensus on the Marshall Plan's adoption—be it from the armed forces, the treasury, or the Congress—many of whom were opposed to Truman and his secretary of State. And yet, the Marshall plan was obstinately carried through one step at a time, funded, and in the end successfully culminated reconstructing most of Western Europe—at the heart of which was Germany and its industrial complex, which serviced most of the rest of Continental Europe.

Ironically, Eastern European relative passivity (relative of course to Western Europe's Marshall Plan) and caution also faired pretty well in the long term. Is this cautious approach likely to work in the Middle East? Daniel Brumberg recently argued to the contrary,

> *Such caution is born of an unwillingness to antagonize the very Arab leaders whose support in the "war against terrorism" the administration seeks. It also reflects anxiety about the growing influence of illiberal Islamists who are waiting to hijack liberal reforms. The result is predictable. Take a look at the State Department's Middle East Partnership Initiative (MEPI) and you will find a long-standing emphasis on the usual liberalization formula: economic reform, promotion of women's rights and the building of civil society. These piecemeal reform programs are designed not to tinker with the fundamental ruling institutions. If Bush is serious, his administration will have to break with these policies and address the heart of the problem: the institutions and ideologies of Arab states."*

What all of this means is that if one looks at recent developments—while perhaps not all concerted—there seems to be a trend of adopting policies somewhere in the middle between a massive policy and a passive one. This was alluded to recently in an article by Washington Post's Robin Wright and Glen Kessler, when they stated that,

*"In stark contrast to the president's four powerful speeches this
year pledging to promote democracy in the Middle East, the Bush
administration has settled on a combination of gentle nudging
and modest funding to achieve its ambitious goals..." Of course the
ambitious goals are those of democratizing the region. The gentle
nudging and modest funding- particularly through initiatives
such as the Middle East Partnership Initiative, MEPI- whose
funding at close to US$120 million annually- point towards a more
passive role, and one firmly in second place behind the Arab-Israeli
Process, which has yielded annual USAID funds to Israel and
the Egyptians in the excess of US$5 billion annually. As Marina
S. Ottaway, co-director of the Democracy Project at the Carnegie
Endowment for International Peace stated, "For a government
that talks so robustly about democracy in the Mideast, the project
takes a low-key and long-term view of the democratic transition."*

This said, it is just as difficult to over-stress passivity when there are almost
200,000 coalition troops on the ground in Iraq; when military costs could
ultimately exceed hundreds of billions of Dollars and when close to US$32
billion have already been earmarked by international donor in a conference
held to fund the reconstruction of Iraq. Also of note have been free trade
agreements pushed through with countries such as Jordan and Morocco
(bilateral with the United States), not to mention Lebanon and Syria's Euro
Med basin accords.

All this leads one to believe that the role that the International
community is bound to play in the liberalization of the Middle East will
not likely be as massive as it was during Western Europe's Marshall Plan
nor as passive as it was for Eastern Europe towards the end of the 1980's. It
is likely to be somewhere in the middle.

My own guess for how this support will play out is it will be multi-
pronged. First and foremost, there will be the integrated liberalization
efforts in Iraq by the Coalition. Iraq will continue to be the center of focus
so as to make a liberalization and democratization success story, which the
Coalition hopes to showcase to the rest of the region. Here, failure is truly

no option to the International Community, because a dismembered Iraq prone to terrorism would be just as intolerable as a return to autocratic Iraq would be. Second there will be economic initiatives by the United States and Europe with Arab nations. These trade agreements in the short term will flush out regional inefficiencies. As these inefficiencies emerge, political aperture becomes inevitable. And so, the agreements will be much more than just trade agreements and will sooner or later become vehicles for the liberalization and democratization of the region. Here also, multinational NGO's such as the World Bank and the IMF will be instrumental, for as economic inefficiencies begin to surface, they will likely be called to do much of the ground work.

Already, both institutions have strong presence in the Levant and North Africa. The World Bank is said to be considering a loan in the amount of US$3 to US$5 billion to Iraq. Third and perhaps more importantly than the other two will be the International Community's role in solving the Israeli-Palestinian deadlock. Already a quartet formed of the United States, Russia, the European Union, and the United Nations have drawn-up a roadmap for peace, whose mission has been announced as the following:

The Quartet will assist and facilitate implementation of the plan, starting in Phase I, including direct discussions between the parties as required...The plan establishes a realistic timeline for implementation... However, as a performance-based plan, progress will require and depend upon the good faith efforts of the parties, and their compliance with each of the obligations outlined below... Should the parties perform their obligations rapidly, progress within and through the phases may come sooner than indicated in the plan... Non-compliance with obligations will impede progress... A settlement, negotiated between the parties, will result in the emergence of an independent, democratic, and viable Palestinian state living side by side in peace and security with Israel and its other neighbors.

On this front, unfortunately the roadmap has been stalling since its launch in mid-2003, and it will likely remain on the back burner until after the

United States elections in 2004. After the elections, however, once again it is likely to occupy a priority for the US administration.

Fourth, there will be a continuation of efforts to democratize the region using a "carrot and sticks strategy". A clear example of this was the recent unanimous congressional passing of the Syrian Accountability act, which "stipulates economic and diplomatic sanctions on Damascus, including a ban on U.S. companies to operate in Syria and reducing diplomatic representation" unless Syria "restrains militants who operate in the country, withdraws its army from Lebanon, and stops its alleged chemical and biological weapons programs". Soon after, however, a moderate American ambassador was appointed to Syria and large oil investments by US companies totaling some US$600 million were announced, leading one analyst to state, "The signing by a U.S. company of the oil exploration contract with Syria after the endorsement of the Accountability Act carried a clear political message that U.S. investments at least might be excluded from the sanctions stipulated under the Act...".

Fifth, there will be institutional support by the international community so as to make sure that once democratization begins, it cannot institutionally falter. As one analyst wrote,

With greater awareness and a deliberate strategy, the international community could do much more to facilitate and solidify democratic transitions, prevent destabilization of democracy, and restore democracy when one institution in a country intrudes on another....[14]

While this may have implications of sovereignty, many precedents in Latin America and Eastern Europe make this less contentious than it used to be. It is time for the international community to stop being passively shy and instead adopt a more proactive democratic approach. It is to their benefit; and it is certainly to the benefit of the entire Arab region.

---

14 Andreas Schedler, Larry Jay Diamond, Marc F. Plattner, the Self-Restraining State, 1999, pg. 124.

Section Three:
Cedar Revolution
(2005-2010)

SECTION THREE:
CEDAR REVOLUTION
(2005-2010)

The year after the United States' invasion of Iraq, the Arab world began seeing major shifts in the regional geopolitical scene. The 800-pound gorilla had invaded one of the major Arab countries, unseated its dictator, and occupied it. The regional chessboard was never going to be the same; and Lebanon—ever a geopolitical fault line—would be one of the first to reel from its effects.

During 2004, I had been busy writing my book, Inevitable Democracy in the Arab World, with most of my focus on the Arab region as a whole and not just Lebanon. And yet whenever I visited my native country, I found it economically and politically gridlocked. The government reconstruction boom that I had witnessed a handful of years earlier had come to a screeching halt weighed down by massive debt servicing. Following IMF guidelines to obtain some debt relief from the international community would practically rob the Lebanese state of any fiscal tools at its disposal as it introduced draconian austerity measures. This was accompanied by a self-imposed dollarization policy, which had the Central Bank defend the Lebanese Lira tooth and nail against any mention of devaluation. "Our dollarization policy has been a keystone to our economic recovery," Riad Salameh had once stated to me back in 2000 in a brief interview held at the Central Bank.

Unfortunately, it also meant that with fiscal constraints already in place, the government did not have much of a monetary policy at its disposal either. At the time, monthly reports on the central bank's foreign currency reserves showed them to be dangerously dwindling. It would all come to a head in 2006 when the Central Bank reserves almost ran out—the saving grace being emergency deposits made by Saudi Arabia and other Gulf countries.

"Reconstructing downtown Beirut has not helped me in the least," some would answer when I enquired about how they were doing. They were of course complaining about the lack of any development outside of the confines of downtown Beirut, which by then had been rebuilt. They claimed the entire post-war reconstruction plan proved to be skewed and did not benefit the people. In one conversation I had with a former Lebanese minister of economy, he argued that most of the projects only served the highest economic echelons and not the people in general; and that Lebanon had effectively become a country by the rich, for the rich, and of a lot of poor. "In Lebanon, there is no middle class anymore," some moaned. Others began to see the role of the Lebanese state—which during the reconstruction phase to a certain degree had been regaining prominence—quickly dissipating. One satirical show on TV portrayed this general sentiment with one phrase, "Wayniyyeh el Dawleh?" meaning "Where the heck is the government?"

At the time, I felt that many Lebanese were groping in the dark not realizing why and what was happening to their nation. In a democracy, one would expect media reporting to shed light on issues. Unfortunately, in Lebanon by then, most media companies had become privatized acting as mouthpieces to the special interest that owned them. The Lebanese would find no bliss in their ignorance, and slowly but surely, they once again relapsed into their sectarian addiction trying to seek answers to their problems from the very same leaders that had been pushing them strong dosages of sectarianism all throughout the civil war. This was very disappointing to so many fellow Lebanese expats all over the world. Having left Lebanon years earlier, we had come to shun sectarianism and the leaders who preached it. We had seen the light of good governance and equal citizenship.

In one conversation I had with one Lebanese newspaper editor at the time, I expressed my concern of rising sectarianism led by leaders whose only interest was self-perpetuation. He dismissed my concern stating that Lebanon's identity was very much sectarian and that this would never change because, as he explained, Lebanon's communities would face extinction.

I was deeply disappointed that people with such prominent voices could not see that a nation divided along sectarian interests will always be unstable, as Lebanon's history has repeatedly shown. This becomes all the more acutely tragic if one considers that the Lebanese constitution itself—in its three amendments since independence—has expressly stated that sectarianism is an ill that should be eliminated. Ironically, many years later, the editor himself would begin complaining himself, and wondering why Lebanon was witnessing such a dangerous rise in sectarianism.

Political gridlock accompanied its economic sibling with two major camps emerging. The first camp blamed the country's woes on economic mismanagement and corruption. The accusing camp was led by the president of the republic who blamed it on wastage by the cabinet headed by the prime minister.[15] The president's camp included some Christians and Shiite groups, including Hezbollah; which of course was fully supported by the Syrian regime and Iran. In talking with people from this camp, I found that their grievances included growing poverty levels and mediocre government service. "In the past, we had no choice but to accept it. Now we don't," they would say.

The other camp was led by Prime Minister Hariri, a Sunni, some other Christian groups led by Michel Aoun, and the Druze community led by Walid Jumblatt. This camp was supported by Saudi Arabia and the West. Their concern was that a viable state could not be built if the other camp insisted on its rejectionism and war-mongering especially after the Israeli withdrawal of 2000. "How could we solve our economic calamity if we have a war every other year?" they asked.

On September 2, 2004, local gridlock would lead to an internationalization of the Lebanese crisis when the United Nations' Security Council passed Resolution 1559.[16] The fact that the resolution was co-sponsored by France and the United States was interesting enough—as it had managed to reunite

---

15 In Lebanon the executive branch is actually split in two, the president and the prime minister, who may or may not be aligned when it comes to policy.

16 During the 1960's Lebanon had a wise president by the name of Fouad Shehab. He realized the dangers inherent in internationalizing Lebanon's politics and how divisive it would be internally to the nation. As a result, in his entire presidency, not once did he leave the country to visit any other in fear of being perceived as being impartial. Even when the powerful Abdel Nasser beckoned him, Shehab agreed to meet him on condition it would be on a tent positioned on the exact border line between Lebanon and Syria. It is said that President Shehab still sat on the Lebanese side of the line.

their regional interests after a serious rift over the Iraqi War. Resolution 1559's objective was first to reaffirm "Lebanon's sovereignty, territorial integrity, unity, and political independence under the sole and exclusive authority of the Government of Lebanon throughout the country." To assure this, the Security Council called for the "disbanding and disarmament of all Lebanese and non-Lebanese militias... [and] for all parties concerned to cooperate fully and urgently with the Council for the full implementation of all its resolutions concerning the restoration in Lebanon of territorial integrity, full sovereignty and political independence."[17]

In Lebanon, the conflicting political players saw this pivotal resolution from two different and diametrically opposed perspectives. The first group supported it and asked for all foreign forces to exit Lebanon—meaning Syria primarily— and for the disarmament of any remaining militias—meaning Hezbollah. The opposing group led by Hezbollah was vehemently against 1559 arguing that it was an attempt to weaken Lebanon's resistance in its stand against Israel. By forcing its foreign-supported backbone—meaning the Syrians—out of Lebanon and the disarmament of the Lebanese resistance, they argued that it served no one but Israel's interests. Besides, they added, this was a domestic issue that was none of the international community's business.

The ensuing chasm between the two camps culminated in treachery and finger pointing. It did not help matters at the time that President Lahoud and Hezbollah were so obviously allied with the Syrian regime and Iran respectively. It did not help either that some were claiming that Hariri himself had covertly been Resolution 1559's primary architect, 'Who else in Lebanon and the region garnered such international support from the French, Americans, and Arabs to have been able to get it done?' they asked. It did not help that then French President Jacque Chirac was a very close friend and ally of Hariri and American President Bush a staunch Saudi ally, as was Hariri himself.

The nation hoped that gridlock would be finally overcome with the end of Lahoud's term in 2004. Disappointment ensued as Lahoud's term was

---

17 http://www.un.org/News/Press/docs/2004/sc8181.doc.htm

extended by parliament in what many claimed was blatant Syrian coercion to keep 'their man' in his position. For his part, Hariri having lost hope in being able to govern together with Lahoud, decided on October 20, 2004 to submit his government's resignation. Unlike what many thought as throwing-in the political towel, Hariri was attempting to politically outflank the president by going directly to the Lebanese people through the upcoming parliamentary elections scheduled for the summer of 2005. He would never get that chance.

On a beautifully serene and sunny Valentine's Day, a one ton bomb-laden truck exploded on a Beirut beach boulevard obliterating Hariri's passing convoy and instantly killing him and some thirty others. It shook the nation, shocked the region, and startled the world—not least France and the United States, who would soon interpret it as a Syrian response to UN Resolution 1559.

As it did to many other Lebanese all over the globe, the assassination of Hariri deeply shocked me. I was never much into idolizing politicians, but I had felt Hariri was unique in that he had risen from nothing to absolute riches and yet had preferred to come back and spend the remaining years of his life helping his war-torn nation get back on its feet. It was not easy for him, as Hariri was torn between working from within a divisive national system, and trying to fix it with outside help. Notwithstanding many of the corrupt allegations that would be hurled at several of his administrations, Hariri persisted in his efforts for more than a decade.

I had met the man on three occasions, one of which was a full-fledged interview in Beirut during the summer of 2000. At the time, I had studied his record, researched his successes and failures, and interviewed some of his top ministers—including the finance and economics ministers. While I could not prove or disprove the corruption charges laid against his administrations, objectively speaking my conclusions pointed more towards fiscal mismanagement due to overly optimistic economic assumptions and volatile geoeconomic conditions than anything else. During that interview, I recall asking Hariri, what he thought about being ousted from power back in 1998 (he had been out of power for two years). His reply still rings in my ear to this day: "The country sent me home in 1998 because I was not doing my job right. And now (meaning in 2000), I am working hard with my team to get back and find new ways to serve the Lebanese people again."

I always felt that a former prime minister of his accomplishments, wealth, and international stature need not have answered this question in this rather self-deprecating manner—that is not unless he truly believed it. And so apart from his administrations' shortfalls, I felt that he deserved credit for his efforts. In the very least, he did not deserve such an incinerating end. And so together with what proved to be millions of fellow Lebanese, I mourned his loss and feared for the future of the country.

At the time, I felt a strong urge to go back and visit. I soon travelled back to Lebanon and visited his resting place in downtown Beirut. On February 26, 2005, less than two weeks after his assassination, I joined hands with thousands of fellow Lebanese in a peaceful human chain that stretched from the bombing site in Beirut's Corniche to where he had been laid to rest.

This chain and several events that followed inspired me to write several commentaries. By then, I had reached the conclusion that only the Lebanese people had the true power to bring about change in Lebanon—and they needed to do it collectively. This rationalization was not so much philosophical as it was Realpolitik. After all, if an executive as powerful as Hariri could not effectuate the desired change and was decimated in an instant, who else could? It certainly wasn't going to be the Lebanese parliamentarians who had proven time-and-again to be coercible into taking positions not necessarily favoring the nation or the people. Nor was it going to be the different leaders, who seemed intent on staying in power no matter what the costs to the country were. So, I rationalized, the only remaining hope for Lebanon going forward was with the people. Little could I have imagined what would actually transpire, which is worthy of many a history book. Suffice it to say that the day the Lebanese people claimed back the power of the state—albeit temporarily—was a day to remember; one which I have since argued was the first post-Iraq Arab Revolution, and the spiritual beginning of the Arab Spring.

The Cedar Revolution, as it would become called, was a seminal event in which Lebanese people from all walks of life took to the streets peacefully and in massive numbers. On March 14, 2005, almost a million people marched into Beirut's downtown area; to force the world to hear their message. It was unprecedented since the days of Abdel Nasser in the Egypt of the 1960s. What was different in Lebanon's case, however, was that the people were not following blindly some iconic leader—the movement itself was actually leaderless—rather it was the common purpose of reclaiming their own destiny.

In a piece I published at the time, I called it Lebanon's "Silent Majority". To me this represented the true Lebanon. People from all regions, social classes, and sects. Not politicians, just regular folks who usually went about their ways without making too much of a fuss. With Hariri's assassination, they felt their future being threatened and collectively decided to congregate and peacefully ask for redress. Compared to the loud thumps being heard in the streets of Baghdad at the time, Beirut's message was soft; yet quite ironically, it was louder, more powerful, and it was instantly heard around world.

Alas this momentous occasion would be followed by many ups and downs. While Syria did withdraw all its troops from Lebanon, political assassinations would continue unabated for the better part of the next two years. Then in 2006, Israel decided to invade Lebanon once more to try and eradicate the Lebanese resistance. It failed in its mission, but succeeded in causing untold human carnage and material damage. The Lebanese, uncertain of whom to blame for their never ending calamity, began pointing the finger at one another intensifying internal division. Instead of collectively uniting to draw a better future for their children, they recoiled once again into divisive sectarian politics, behind pretty much the same leaders and movements they had followed for the previous three decades.

When I reflect upon some of my writings during this period, I cannot help but marvel at the Lebanese revolutionary accomplishment, while despairing at the eventual pitfalls; and at how some Lebanese continued to prefer defining themselves and their politics through a prism of differences as opposed to one of commonalities. Perhaps living overseas helped me, and others like me, weed out more easily the noise of local petty politics and see things for what they were. Critics may argue that these very ideas oversimplify Lebanese and regional complexities. I asked the question from the exact opposite perspective. Could it not be that some in Lebanon tended to over-complicate rather straight-forward issues?

To me the power of the Lebanese Cedar Revolution of 2005 speaks for itself. The people rose as a collective and peacefully effectuated unprecedented change in the shortest time possible. Not one bullet was fired. It was done in the most respectful, dignified, and thoughtful manner. And while a sizeable swathe of Lebanon's population did not participate, they did not actively oppose it either, eventually allowing for change to occur.

I continue to believe, more now than ever, that only the Lebanese people will be able to force change for their own good. Only they and no one else can build a better future once and for all, circumventing a repeat of the nation's tragic history. But they cannot do it as sects any more than they could do it as individuals. They could only do it by acting in a unified manner as they did during the Cedar Revolution. While, it won't be easy, the good news is that they have already proven that they are capable of doing it.

Until that day comes, the true Cedar Revolution remains a work in progress ...

Technocratizing Lebanon? Why not start with the tech sector? (September 2004)[18]

Lately and as a result of the political debate traversing Lebanon, there has been much discussion on technocratizing government—i.e. depoliticizing some government functions in favor of specialists and experts working within the confines of institutions. Here's a no-brainer starting point—Lebanon's High Tech (ICT) sector.

In Lebanon, we have come a long way in ICT. In 1992, the telecom infrastructure was in a shambles and we had an estimated 250,000 badly maintained phone lines serving a population of more than 3 million. We did not have any mobile telephony. The business sector had little if any investments in IT. The government itself conducted its operations mostly

---

18   First published by Daily Star, MENA FN, and the Potsdam eGovernment Competence Center on September 23, 2004.

based on pen and paper—if at all (I remember one MP closely involved with the budget process back then describing to me that the budget documents used to arrive to the Ministry of Finance (MOF) bounded with a rope typically used for fruit boxes). Schools and universities considered technology a luxury and in fact half of the private schools and all of the public schools had no technology as late as 1996 as per a study conducted by AUB... But that was then...

Today, as with all major sectors, ICT in Lebanon has advanced by leaps and bounds. A state of the art fixed line network was installed in the mid-1990's capable of handling about 1.2 million lines. A cellular network grew beyond projections serving some 700,000 clients. The government itself, due to the good offices of OMSAR, the MOF, Lebanon's Central Bank, and others, and with international technical assistance, actually led the private sector in the mid-1990's with technology adoption yielding excellent results in areas such as customs automation, cadaster, national archives, not to mention the security apparatus. Over the past two years there has also been much talk about jump-starting e-gov initiatives.

While there has been good advances, ICT in Lebanon is far from reaching its potential, and seems to have fallen behind the likes of Jordan and Egypt. There is one basic reason for this—lack of institutionalized government ICT sponsorship—as opposed to ad hoc ICT projects. In a study conducted for Harvard University in 2002, titled *Institutionalizing National ICT Strategies: The Case of Lebanon*, the main conclusions reached were that Lebanon's primary ICT strength was in its abundance of highly qualified human resources—as compared to regional nations such as Jordan, for instance. Lebanon's entrepreneurial initiative created a bottom-up dynamic that could easily be the envy of advanced places such as Dubai and Malaysia. However, what was found was that Lebanon lacked institutional strategy, support, and guidance for its ICT sector. In other words, whereas nations such as Jordan, Egypt, and UAE had a predominantly top-down approach that sometimes lacked the initiative at the bottom to take advantage of this government support; Lebanon was found to have the opposite problem—complete reliance on the bottom's initiative without much institutionalized support from the top.

That is not to say Lebanon has not tried. In 1997, the Lebanese government saw the need for a national ICT strategy and hired some Anglo consultants to draw up the necessary ICT strategy. The institution delegated to carry out these resulting strategies was OMSAR—which did a lot but constantly found it hard to fully commit given its much more massive (and politicized) responsibility of overall administrative reform. By 1998, with a new government in place whose mantra was tight fiscal controls, the ICT initiatives fell into the lap of the ministry of the economy, industry, and trade. The minister in charge—an economist—changed focus to e-gov and made an honest effort; but there was only so much mindshare that ICT could capture given all his other responsibilities—particularly since most ICT issues—at the infrastructure level—are multi-ministry issues that require not much macro-views and ideas, but rather micro-issues needing ICT experience and understanding in standards, compatibilities, and constantly shifting IT market tendencies. With the government's change in 2000, the ICT ball would fall back once again into OMSAR's court with the same political shackles it had prior adding to serious budgetary restrictions that made any ICT much harder to implement.

It is therefore no surprise that issues such as offering DSL to the Lebanese market—something that according to a study conducted by Microsoft in Lebanon is likely to draw tens of millions of Dollars into the government's coffers—has never taken off. It is no surprise that the plans drawn up with the help of USTDA for a technology park in Dammour several years ago is still a pipe dream. It is no surprise that e-government initiatives that could touch the lives of the citizen are usually delivered in a ministry-specific "island" format as opposed to an overall centralized citizen-centric approach reducing their impact. It is no surprise that ICT strategies set years ago have yet to be implemented even though the ICT assets are already sitting idle and could yield sizeable revenues to a government and a nation in dire need of new sources of income and employment opportunities.

So what to do about it? In the aforementioned Harvard study, the primary recommendation given to solve this problem was to create a quasi-government ICT institution along the lines of arguably the most stable, sturdy, and consistent of Lebanon's institutions—the Lebanese Central Bank.

This may seem grandiose and over-ambitious, but to set the expectations straight. What is being sought with this analogy is not so much magnitude as structure. In its simplest form, the idea is to create an independent and relatively non-politicized institution whose mission it is to support and coordinate all Lebanese ICT initiatives within a strategic framework put together by ICT technocrats and with the participation of the Lebanese government. This would be very much in the general spirit that accompanied the creation of the well-respected Lebanese Central Bank half a century earlier, and which brought together under its auspices the Lebanese Bankers Association, the MOF, and the Council of Ministers. In so doing the nation managed to coordinate the proper monetary strategies and policies, all the while maintaining recognized and respected technocratic independence. The proposed ICT institution needs a similar setup, but it need not be massive in structure. The idea is for it to be lean and efficient sub-contracting studies and coordinating with the different national ICT stakeholders within and outside the government—including ICT infrastructure players such as the telecoms. The idea is for it to also have some regulatory prowess, particularly on issues such as piracy and intellectual property. The direct effect of all this would be a proper and independent ICT institution charged with setting strategy, assuring continuity in deployment and accountability for the results.

Of course the first reaction from some might be 'it is better to let the market function'. Unfortunately it hasn't either in Lebanon or internationally, which is why countries such as Jordan, Egypt, UAE, Malaysia, Singapore, Colombia, and many others have adopted this kind of structure. The next concern might be 'how in the heck would the Lebanese government even afford yet another institution with all the current budgetary problems?' In all fairness, this response is akin to killing the goose that lays the golden egg. According to the MOF, the Lebanese government's second source of income (after taxes) currently comes from ICT (this includes money from the mobile sector and the fixed line networks). If strategies are implemented properly, much more revenue is bound to come—be it from DSL or ISDN bandwidth rents; e-government initiatives which could become revenue-generating as citizens would be willing to pay for higher degrees of efficiency and expediency; other ICT rents from initiatives such as incubators and business accelerators whose funding could also come from international NGO's and donors; not to mention professional IT associations and businesses who might be interested in pitching-in for such an institution for their own benefit (fighting piracy...). Surely, the proposed ICT Institution could be self-funded by allocating a small portion of the marginal benefits received from the sector.

Sounds too easy? It will certainly require institutional building vision, ICT expertise, and overall persistence. But if the government leaders have a genuine desire to technocratize Lebanon, why not start with the tech sector?

Amending Lebanese election laws where it really counts (September 2004)

Lately there has been a lot of a talk about amending Lebanon's election law. The debate has heated-up no doubt with President Lahoud's sudden and controversial re-election. Ironically, it seems that the election-law amendment under discussion has little to do with the presidential election. Rather, it is more focused on parliamentary elections.

The main idea on the table is that of "nationalizing" the parliamentary elections—in other words making Lebanon one district for the parliamentary elections. Essentially, the idea would have a parliamentary candidate, say in the city of Tripoli or one in the Bekaa voted into parliament by the entire registered Lebanese populace regardless of where in the country they actually live or where they are registered to vote. The idea pretty much ends there, and generally does not delve into national elections for any of the executives (premier or president). It also does not address the issue of sectarianism, which according to Lebanon's constitution in its three major amendments (1926, 1943, and 1989) is transitional and needs to be abolished. Therefore, a safe assumption here would be that the election law discussion proposes to only change election district boundaries for parliamentary elections, and would not touch either the executive branch; nor does it aim to abolish sectarianism. With this in mind, let us consider its merits.

The best way to do this is to take a possible scenario and see how it may play out. Say the law was passed for a single parliamentarian election district, there will be a milieu of potential candidates from all national currents submitting their names to a national ballot. A person voting would have to pick 128 out of several hundred candidates (in the 2000 elections, there were more than 500 candidates). The law is then likely to elect the 128 candidates with the most votes. Of course, if the sectarian parliamentary division is to remain (64 Muslim and 64 Christian), then it means that the top 64 of each (and their sub-sectarian composition) would be voted in regardless of the number of total votes.

Here one problem could arise in that a parliamentarian with a lot more popular votes than one from another sect may actually lose out because he did not make the top 64 cut-off—arguably a minor problem if the vote difference is not that much (which is usually the case with smaller districts). However, since it is national in scope, it could turn into a major problem if for instance a parliamentarian with 4,000 votes beats one with 200,000 votes. This is likely to be the case particularly if intra-sect voting occurs. Typically, the counter-argument here is that Lebanon's system was never meant to be majority-based; but if this is the case, then what use is a single district vote to begin with? Would it not be more logical to have each region elect its own MP as is the case today?

But let us take a step back here and see who is likely to become a candidate to begin with (regardless of sect). Here we face another problem, because those likely to become candidates are those with the resources to run national campaigns (or in the very least those allied to them). In other words, Lebanon's political elite will find themselves with an even more sizeable advantage over any candidate without such connections. Is this likely to dissolve Lebanon's political cronyism or is it likely to increase it?

A third problem presents itself with responsibility and accountability. If, say an MP from Sour or Baalbek won a seat in parliament by a national vote, then who will they be responsible to, their local community or Lebanon as a whole? What would happen if, say a candidate received 1,000 local city votes and 150,000 votes from other places in Lebanon, whereas his losing counterpart received 130,000 local votes and 1,000 votes from other parts of Lebanon? Who is more worthy to represent their community? Who is likely to be more responsible and accountable?

Making Lebanon into a single parliamentary-voting district is not politically viable nor in the interest of the Lebanese people, which as-is feel themselves diluted and alienated from the political class representing them. What the Lebanese need is not political gerrymandering benefiting the ruling classes by monopolizing parliamentary elections. Rather, they need a parliament close to their voices and their daily needs. They can only get that if parliamentary elections remain local.

If election re-engineering is the taste of the day and the Lebanese leaders are truly serious about amending the election law, then perhaps they should stop dabbling with parliament for the time being and start where it could really make a difference. Maybe a better place to start would be creating nationwide elections for the executives themselves. Perhaps, this would give these executives the mandate needed to actually manage the affairs of the nation and not live in eternal and senseless gridlock. And if and when they don't perform, then in place of lingering around indefinitely by making this or that deal with apparently easy-to-sway parliamentary blocks, the Lebanese populace would decide by itself and for itself who it wants to lead it!

You just don't kill Hariri (February 15, 2005)

The assassination of Prime Minster Hariri no doubt has shocked Lebanon and Lebanese everywhere. Once the fallout has settled, however, many will be left to ponder and learn from his historic legacy and the meaning of his life for months and years to come. You just don't kill Hariri.

Hariri was one of the very few Lebanese—dare I say Arab—leaders who clearly rose above the fray. Everything about him, from his humble beginnings in the small Lebanese city of Saida, to his amassing of immense wealth in Saudi Arabia, to his international charity work helping fund the education of thousands of Lebanese students during wartime, to his assumption of the Lebanese premiership, makes his journey an epic one. You just don't kill Hariri's journey; you admire it.

Hariri was arguably its most international of leaders, befriending kings, presidents and leaders the world over. At a time when few believed in Lebanon's revival, he managed to pull together the international community through several global conferences attracting the needed attention to Lebanon and its plight. And yet in his heart, Hariri did this because he was nothing but a Lebanese, who believed in his nation, its beauty, its people, and its traditions. You just don't kill Hariri's nationalism; you embrace it.

Hariri's vision from the outset was one of a new Lebanon. Right after the civil war ended, when very few believed in its potential, Hariri was among the first who whole-heartedly immersed himself in the project of raising Lebanon from its civil war ashes. He would dedicate the remainder of his life to this end. While in retrospect, many may criticize some excesses; it is only fair to say that Hariri's vision has been and will continue to be that which guides the nation. You just don't kill Hariri's vision; you build on it.

And yet, Hariri was not only about vision, but leadership. Once in power, he did not rest on his laurels as many had before him. Rather, he got to the work he knew best—building. Often named "The Bulldozer", he bulldozed his way into Lebanon's history books by rebuilding everything from roads, schools, airports, not to mention Lebanon's showpiece—downtown Beirut. You just don't kill Hariri's leadership; you follow it.

Hariri's political views, while sometimes controversial, were generally reconciliatory and democratic. I recall in an interview I had with him in the summer of 2000—the only period until recently in which he had been out of government—I asked him what he thought about being ousted from power. Not one known to mince words, his answer was simple and straightforward, "Many in Lebanon thought my government did not do a good job, and so I was sent home. There is nothing wrong with that, and I have learnt my lessons. It is part of the Lebanese democracy." These words may seem normal in Western culture. Coming from an Arab, a billionaire, and a man who had literally helped engineer the ending of his country's civil war, rebuilt it, and put it back on the global map, it is nothing short of extraordinary. You just don't kill Hariri's humble respect for his nation's democracy; you learn from it.

While Hariri has tragically left our world, it is only in the flesh. His vision, his love of country, his reconciliatory stance, his leadership, and his respect for its democracy will remain. You just don't kill Hariri. No matter who you are, you just don't.

Hariri's death shows the futility of executive sectarianism (February 2005)[19]

Understandably, the first reaction of many Lebanese when they heard news of the assassination of former Prime Minister Rafic Hariri was fear that inter-sectarian strife could re-emerge and possibly lead to civil war. And yet the subsequent national outpouring of grief for the slain leader proved that this was unfounded. Support came from all quarters and cut across all religions and sects. If anything, this proved that sectarianism in Lebanon's executive branch has become an obsolete institution, which does the nation more harm than good.

What leads to this conclusion? Sectarianism probably had little to do with the motive behind the assassination. While Hariri could play sectarian politics every now and then, he was perceived as a national figure. In fact, this past October, when he started leaning toward the opposition in its stand against the government, Hariri effectively abandoned the prospective comfort of a specifically Sunni premiership for a "nationalist" agenda—putting Lebanon ahead of any sectarian political considerations he may have held. This did not escape the attention of the Lebanese public, whose mass presence at his funeral last week confirmed the former prime minister's widespread popularity.

In contrast, right about the time that Hariri's nationalist star may have soared, that of his political rival, President Emile Lahoud, plummeted. If a poll were taken, it is likely to show that the steepest drop in Lahoud's popularity occurred right after his term was extended last fall, which many Lebanese see as having been imposed by Syria because it sought a guarantee against implementation of UN Security Council Resolution 1559 calling

---

19   First published in the Daily Star on February 22, 2005.

for a Syrian withdrawal from Lebanon. In other words, Lahoud's popularity plummeted not because of sectarian considerations, but because he was no longer perceived as being a president representing Lebanese interests, but Syrian ones. Ironically, what little popularity Lahoud now can muster comes mainly from sects other than the Maronites.

All this raises the following question: How relevant is sectarianism at the executive level in Lebanon today? After all, the country is currently not engaged in a sectarian struggle as it was right before the civil war. Unlike the early 1970s, when the Palestinian issue split the Lebanese political system broadly between Muslims and Christians, the current matter of the Syrian presence has not done so. In fact, all sects are represented on both sides of the Syria argument; and the split seems to follow a fault line defined by Lebanese nationalist aspirations.

Sectarianism in the executive has shown its irrelevance, as it did back in 1975, when faced with the potential for civil war the sectarian order was unable to prevent a meltdown. So, of what use is it to Lebanon today? Would it not be better to offer a political safety valve through a non-sectarian popular vote for key executive positions? In retrospect this would have diffused Lahoud's re-election time-bomb and perhaps spared Hariri's life.

It is not surprising that the late Syrian President Hafez Assad repeatedly stressed the importance of eliminating Lebanese executive sectarianism in parallel with a withdrawal of Syrian forces. His reasoning was derived from an assumption that as long as such sectarianism existed in Lebanon, the country would be ripe for discord, strife, and manipulation—not just by Syria but by others as well.

While sectarianism in the executive may seem too entrenched, Lebanese actions over the past few days have proven it otherwise. The Lebanese crave nationalist leaders who transcend sects. Unfortunately the current system cannot provide this, and when it does, the outcome is either gridlock or catastrophe. And so, the Lebanese have a choice to make: Either they can accept an executive branch that is elected directly by the people and uniquely responsible to the people, something difficult to fiddle with from the outside; or they can maintain what they have, which allows outsiders to manipulate the political system.

Which will it be? Given the public's national reaction to Hariri's murder last week, it seems pretty clear that they might prefer to go forward.

Lesson from Chile to Lebanon: Simply vote NO!
(February 2005)

By the late 1980's, Chileans who had been under Pinochet's dictatorship for more than a decade had grown tired of his stifling regime. The Chileans were educated and wanted their freedom; but with the anarchy and coup d'états events of 1973 still fresh on their minds; they did not have the stomach for any revolution or military face-off. Pinochet of course played on this fear, and constantly portrayed the opposing political parties as anarchical. He justified an ever increasing police state with the age old argument that it was for national security. The political parties, for their part, remained splintered, and had different ideologies and agendas—some on the left and some on the right. During the decade after the coup, they had found it very difficult to reproach and create a common opposition—many still carrying grudges from the coup days and blaming one another for having indirectly caused it.

By 1989, Pinochet began feeling the popular heat, and needed to find a way to perpetuate his rule, giving it the mere facetiousness of a democracy. While calling for a plebiscite for an extension, he also tightened political party participation. Pinochet wanted to institutionalize his undisputed rule. Notwithstanding the stifling political environment, the Chilean opposition wisely accepted what little opening it was being given. Besides not having another choice, its leaders thought if they ever would have a chance to dispute Pinochet's rule they needed to do so even by his restricted rules.

What resulted was a battle for the heart and minds of the Chilean population. Pinochet had the muscle and the money, but the opposition had the message: a message of true freedom and democracy to the masses, simplified under one simple banner: NO—meaning no to Pinochet's perpetual rule.

Since October 2004, when President Lahoud's rule was renewed, the Lebanese opposition has been embroiled in a similar political battle. Under pressure and coercion, and while ideologically having different agendas, the Lebanese opposition united under one and one simple banner: NO— meaning no to Syria's continuous presence. The question now becomes how to act on this NO. Will it be through mass demonstrations as those that have been evident after the tragic death of Prime Minister Hariri? Will it be through peaceful mass disobedience? Will it be through an official plebiscite—petitions have already been seen being signed in Beirut around the burial site of Mr. Hariri? Or will action wait until the parliamentary elections to be held in May, upon which time the opposition would seek a vast majority that would render the current government obsolete and futile?

Whatever happens over the next few days and weeks, one thing is almost certain. The Lebanese opposition have united under one national banner, and with the death of Mr. Hariri, they seem to have received the blessing of the masses.

Will Lebanon witness the miracle witnessed in Chile a mere decade ago, when in spite all his muscle, money, and Machiavellian tactics, Pinochet still lost the popular vote to the opposition? For one, the chips seem to be stacked in their favor. Like Chile back in 1989, not only are the popular masses now backing the opposition, but so are the religious authorities, and the international community at large. It remains up to the opposition to maintain its ranks unified under a simple and clear message that everyone can understand and relate to: NO! Mr. Hariri may still witness the political victory he paid his life for.

Syrian withdrawal is not enough (February 2005)

The billowing smoke from the explosion that killed Prime Minister Hariri had not cleared when political finger-pointing began and the issue of 1559 was brought to the fore, calling for Syria's withdrawal from Lebanon. While this has served to unify the Lebanese masses in unprecedented national manifestations, the Lebanese ought to question its solidity and whether its scope is likely to defuse the long term Lebanese political problem.

First, for all we know, Syria may have actually not perpetrated the crime. Their ineptitude and that of their Lebanese proxies could have allowed others to do it for them; and in the process checkmate them into leaving Lebanon. The question, however, is even if innocence were proven by the international investigators that are about to arrive to Beirut, will it all of a sudden defuse Lebanese calls for Syrian withdrawal? The answer to this is: no. In fact, withdrawal calls began even before Prime Minister Hariri was assassinated. Rather, there were national dynamics already in place leading to this call. Hariri's murder essentially was the needle that broke the camel's back. This should not translate into de-legitimizing the call for withdrawal, but rather into avoiding the potential pitfall of placing the entire political bet on whether or not Syria was guilty of the perpetrated crime.

This said, what seems to be much more relevant is the massive Lebanese movement, which with unprecedented unity is calling for its own will to be obeyed. This is much more fundamental, and has little to do with Syria. In other words, while the Syrian government may declare its innocence—and were the Lebanese and international community to give them the benefit of the doubt—it's obsolete regime's archaic voice will hardly be heard against the clear message being sent to the world by the renascent Lebanese popular voice.

And so, for the first time in years, there is a shift in the power dynamics from Damascus back to Beirut. In other words, the Lebanese people are well on their way to fully retaining the mastership over their own destiny. And so the question facing us Lebanese now is what political mechanism do we have to constructively channel this newly found popular will; and is our current political system ready for this new power base?

Unfortunately, there is no mechanism at this moment that channel's the people's direct voice, except for the parliamentary vote. The parliament, however, lost much of its credibility last September, when it was manipulated into no less than a constitutional amendment extending the term of an unpopular president. Waiting until May's election, is also likely to be a feeble attempt to defuse the people's anger at having been deprived from their national aspiration as represented by Hariri's murder. Besides, even if the parliamentary election were to produce a resounding victory for the opposition, President Lahoud, whose popularity and credibility are at rock bottom would remain in place for another three years exercising the same contentious military and intelligence powers regardless of the nation's will. And since he is a staunch supporter of Syria, even were Syria to withdraw its troops to alleviate international pressure, it would continue to exercise immense power in Lebanon through its Lebanese proxies.

It seems that what is now required in Lebanon is something much more fundamental than a mere Syrian withdrawal matched with a business-as-usual easily manipulated parliamentarian system. Rather, what is required is a Lebanese popular affirmation of the executives themselves. This essentially means the establishment of a national vote of confidence for the nation's entire executive branch and that includes both the president and cabinet. While some may attack this as being incitingly violating the Ta'ef accord, it surely would not be the first. In the very least, its objective is channeling the Lebanese people's voice as our constitution unquestionably ought to.

The world is looking at us. It is time we took our destiny back into our own hands; and once and for all took true ownership and absolute responsibility of our independent national will. This requires much more than just a Syrian pull-out. It requires the people's ability to vote-in or throw out the president or the Cabinet if and when it feels that such a government has been inept or has worked against its national interest. Nothing less than full power to the Lebanese people ought to quell Lebanese aspirations.

Go for direct Lebanese elections to avoid outside manipulation (March 2005) [20]

The Lebanese opposition scored a historic victory when the government of Omar Karami resigned earlier this week. And yet it also warned this was only the beginning. This raises a question as to where the end is. Is it changing the electoral law? Is it forcing the resignation of President Emile Lahoud? Is it forcing Syria out of Lebanon? Is it disarming Hezbollah? All these questions are important, but there is also a more fundamental question that few people seem to be asking: Who will decide?

---

20 First published in the Daily Star on March 4, 2005.

As a result of former Prime Minister Rafic Hariri's assassination, state power in Lebanon has shifted dramatically from the executive branch to parliament. Already, the 1989 Ta'ef Accord, which formally placed executive power in the Council of Ministers, split the executive branch and made sure that a weakened president and the prime minister competed for power, rendering both offices much less effective. Hariri overshadowed this to a certain extent and was undeniably the country's most powerful prime minister since Ta'ef. Unfortunately, Ta'ef without Hariri will be very different than Ta'ef was with him. Proof of this is the fact that the governments Hariri did not head during the past 13 years were short-lived. This volatile dynamic is unlikely to change in the future.

From a practical perspective, what all this means is that after Hariri most political decision-making authority will now rest in the Lebanese Parliament. Unfortunately, such a sectarian and fractured body does not have enough cohesiveness for proper long-term policymaking, let alone implementation. Its structure has also not allowed it to be immune from endemic outside manipulation, leading to calamitous decisions.

For instance, it was parliament that voted to extend Lahoud's term in September 2004. Subsequently, it voted confidence (with an unimpressive margin) in Prime Minster Karami's government. And had it been left to parliament, it would have reaffirmed this confidence had Karami not resigned first, notwithstanding the government's utter incompetence following Hariri's murder. Fortunately, Karami's decision avoided humiliating Lebanon's only standing democratic institution.

And so a fundamental question is raised: Have the Lebanese perhaps given too much power to their Parliament and, in the process, accidentally mortgaged their political future?

Some may argue that the parliament is but a manifestation of the political will of the Lebanese people. Yet this has not always proven to be the case. The extension of Lahoud's term last year was a classic example of how the Lebanese were second-guessed by a legislature manipulated by Syria. At the time, other candidates in the Maronite community would have likely received much more popular support than the president. Similarly, the confirmation of Karami's Cabinet was yet another show of parliamentary acquiescence. In retrospect, had there been a popular election pitting Hariri against Karami, few Lebanese in their right mind would have placed their national aspiration in the latter.

The great worry in the future is that an incoherent legislature may continue to be manipulated into acting against the popular will by choosing disliked and ineffective presidents and prime ministers. Will Lebanon be doomed to recycling mediocre leaders, so different from the effective Hariri? The answer to such questions ultimately depends on whether the Lebanese people continue to primarily delegate the choice of their leaders to the parliament or whether they seek to institutionalize their democratic will—clearly demonstrated of late on the streets of Downtown Beirut—by demanding to choose their national executive directly.

The goal here is not to cloud the message of the recent popular demonstrations, but rather to find ways to institutionalize what they represent. Chanting for Syrian withdrawal is fine but not enough. If truth be told, even were the Syrians to exit soon, and hopefully they will, this would not resolve Lebanon's structural political problems. The Lebanese must amend the system by which they are governed in order to hedge against outsiders picking their leaders. Manipulating an entire population is far more difficult than doing so 128 politicians.

Now that the political field has been leveled by Hariri's assassination, nothing short of the Lebanese people's direct empowerment to choose their executive through a democratically competitive process will provide the latter with a national mandate. Nothing less than such a mandate will give the nation the true leadership and unity crucial to face impending national challenges—including issues as potentially divisive as the disarmament of Hezbollah and Palestinian groups, not to mention addressing the problems of the teetering economy.

And nothing less than direct elections ought to satisfy the aspirations of all those currently raising the Lebanese flag in Beirut's Martyrs' Square.

The roaring sound of silence in Lebanon (March 2005)[21]

Last week, many government loyalists in Lebanon thought their manifestation—the one organized and led by Hezbollah—had finally quelled the opposition into quiet submission. The subsequent reappointment of Prime Minister Karami to head the government—notwithstanding his humiliating departure a couple of weeks earlier—was meant to be the nail in the opposition's coffin. Few in Lebanon's already precarious leadership—or that of Syria for that matter—had any clue of the national manifestation it would lead to—one whose magnitude arguably has not been seen in the Arab world since the days of Egypt's Nasser. But who was it that moved, why did they move, what is different about them, and more importantly what do they want?

Unlike Hezbollah's organized manifestation that occurred a week ago, the organization of this manifestation was voluntary, national, and non-party based; and it moved the one and only part of the Lebanese population that had hitherto rarely been driven towards mobilization—that of the "Silent Majority".

The "Silent Majority" in Lebanon is not sectarian in nature. It represents Lebanon's entire spectrum in terms of sects as well as regions including the North, South, Bekaa, coastal cities, and of course the capital, Beirut. This "Silent Majority" is Lebanese and lives in Lebanon; but it is internationally aware, has access to the outside world—either through the media, immigration, relatives, friends, or business relationships. Demographically, it includes both sexes and ages; but a large portion is composed of Lebanon's young—many of whom were witnesses to Lebanon's vicious civil war.

Lebanon's "Silent Majority" also spreads across all Lebanon's economic classes. It is fairly educated and developed. It understands and is concerned about Lebanon's economic predicament and the debt sword hanging over Lebanon's head. While it may not be wealthy, it is ambitious and realizes that for any economic recovery to be sustainable there needs to be political

---

21 First published in the Daily Star on March 17, 2005.

and economic stability coupled with hard work and sacrifices; and in the recent past, it has been willing to quietly pay its fair share.

For the most part, the "Silent Majority" is politically neutral—and until now many thought apathetic; for it watches boisterous leaders parade by, but has hardly ever moved. It does not support any single party in Lebanon because Lebanon's parties are quite splintered and sectarian in nature—a system which in its very nature alienates the "Silent Majority". It prefers nationalists; alas Lebanon's political sectarian system hinders it. Internationally, while it may believe in certain causes, it has etched in its memory the bitter war experiences it paid for by shouldering others' causes. No longer swayed by regional banners, it has become practical enough to realize that Lebanon can no longer afford to be a proxy in regional wars nor face-off points with the likes of Israel. And while Lebanon's "Silent Majority" may shirk from signing a peace deal with Israel, they do not preach for war with it either.

So, why did this "Silent Majority" move"? Quite simply: They are tired! They are tired of seeing their moderate and visionary executives assassinated, only to be left to the mercy of visionless leaders appointed by outsiders and who cannot see beyond their own archaic and provincial eyesight—let alone execute an inch more than they are instructed to. They are tired of having a clueless government who does not represent their interests nor owe them allegiance, particularly at such a crucial time in the nation's history when so many dark clouds are hovering over and are about to rain-in a national disaster. And they are tired of bowing their heads while having to tell their children that it is best to leave their nation's shores in search of a better future.

While some may claim that Lebanon is unique, the national manifestation has shown that Lebanon's "Silent Majority" is not so different from its counterparts elsewhere in the world—as Chile's, for instance, which brought down the all-powerful Pinochet having gotten tired of his repressive police state and his self-serving and obsolete security warnings. It is not so different from its counterparts in Eastern Europe who brought down their own oppressive and manipulative governments who had led them to economic ruin, while their moderate and peaceful neighbors were well on their way to economic prosperity. And, it is not so different from Iraq, which bravely showed the world how powerful the voice of freedom can be—even while facing the direst of personal risks.

No, Lebanon's "Silent Majority" is not unique, for it wants the same thing that all humans everywhere want: dignity, freedom, and peace. It wants a vision of the Lebanon, which is economically ambitious, entrepreneurial and prosperous. It will follow those offering this optimistic vision; and it will dwarf those who wish to bind Lebanon to its dark past through strategies that do not match the above vision. It wants to choose governments who can execute on this vision while wearing the red white and green flag, and with little if any consideration to any other.

The "Silent Majority" in Lebanon has spoken with a roar that has silenced everyone else; and in this has taken the nation's destiny into its own hands. Those in power had better yield and quickly.

Lebanon's political ceilings, floors, and the dues in between (April 2005)[22]

A new addition to the political lexicon in Lebanon these days is what many politicians are referring to as the political "ceiling". By this, they figuratively mean to say political aspirations. It is now common to hear—and particularly from the opposition—that their political ceiling is that of the Ta'ef accord—an accord which was signed in 1989 by the Lebanese warring factions ushering in a return to civil peace. Of course, when these politicians discuss this "ceiling", they are essentially aiming to do two things. First, house the opposition under this ceiling, and second make it clear to Syria that once it leaves; they will respectfully abide by much of what the accord stipulated—most notably the "special" relations with Syria.

In this, however, the opposition may be over-stepping the Lebanese people's desire. First off, the Ta'ef is not nor was it ever meant to be either an end or a ceiling to Lebanon's political aspirations. Rather, it was a means for the return of normality. Ta'ef was a means to disarm the different

---

22 First published in the Daily Star on April 8, 2005.

groups for the reestablishment of peaceful co-existence within the different communities. It was a means to stabilize the nation by having Lebanon and Syria coordinate foreign policy—at a time when Israel was still occupying a very large portion of southern Lebanon. This arguably made good sense and was in the interest of Lebanon—and even Syria—in 1989.

We are now in 2005—four years short of a 20 year anniversary of Ta'ef. Israel withdrew from most of Lebanon in 2000 with the exception of the disputed Shebaa farms, which even Hezbollah—Israel's arch nemesis—seems optimistic that it will be withdrawn from soon. Internally, Lebanon's political and security system deficiencies, once thought of as having been rebuilt, have been exposed by non-other than the United Nations in the Fitzgerald report as having been manipulated and debilitated by Syrian hegemony. As a result, Syria is now well on its way out of Lebanon. All the while, Lebanon's debt-ridden economy, which was beginning to show signs of take-off, is now simmering having been brought to the brink by the loss of confidence resulting from Hariri's assassination and the subsequent bombings. Under these circumstances, no one in Lebanon, not even the opposition, has the right to promise anyone—not even Syria—what Lebanon's political ceiling will be. It is unnecessary, untimely, and will not be accepted by the Lebanese masses.

Instead of talking about ceilings, perhaps it may be better to talk about a "floor" or a base, on which a democratic and prosperous Lebanese society could be constructed. Indeed, the Ta'ef's explicit recognition for the need to eliminate sectarianism from the political sphere is in itself proof positive of how its framers were positioning it as a base; for this alone will require fundamental rethinking across the board in Lebanon from the establishment of national political parties, to institutional restructuring, not to mention foreign policy formulation. These challenges are daunting enough to be constrained by setting false political ceilings or promising it to others.

But if the Ta'ef is not the ceiling, then what will be? And equally important why have the politicians in Lebanon—even the opposition—not fully realized it yet, and when will they?

To answer the first question, and circumventing any pious arguments, the only political ceiling that should exist in Lebanon hereon forward is that of the democratic will of the people. This means the Lebanese people themselves should determine whether there will be a ceiling and if so what this ceiling is and if and when it should change. So, instead of trying to guess what the ceiling is, it may be wiser to find the proper democratic mechanisms needed for the Lebanese people to figure them out on their own in a civil and institutionalized manner.

The second question is why have many of the current politicians not realized this and when will they? Some have admittedly been very surprised by the massive civil manifestations. Arguably, it will take them time to internalize the full institutional implications. Other politicians have been ruled over for years if not decades; and so not unlike the prisoner whose jailer has left with the doors open, they may find it difficult to take that first step out of their political cell for fear of the unknown. It will take them time to adjust to the new realities emerging where the will of the people actually rules. Of course, some may simply never adjust and will just wither away in political consternation. It may even take a younger generation of Lebanese politicians from the mobilized populace to break old habits.

In the meantime, everyone must be very careful not to commit the nation to more dues. Lebanon simply has no will nor the ability to pay; for it has paid more than its fair share in life, limb, prosperity, and forgone tranquility and happiness. The younger generation, whose childhood was kidnapped during the civil war, already has its work cut out for it having to foot the hefty $30 billion ransom for many years to come.

So, with all due respect to many of the opposition politicians' brave stand, now is no time to construct any false ceilings. And if they attempt to, they may soon find themselves in not too dissimilar a position from today's beleaguered government—whose own ceiling is about to cave in.

Time for women to vote for women in the Arab world (May 2005)

On a recent trip to Dubai, I saw in the paper a picture of a sullen woman sitting alone in what seemed like a large and empty conference hall. Turns out the woman was sitting in Kuwait's parliamentary hall where a decision had been made shortly before not to allow women to vote. The look on her face said it all... utter disappointment!

How to deal with this issue? While I am not sure if I am the most qualified to speak on behalf of Arab women, here are some suggestions...

To begin with, they should not be deterred from carrying on with their cause for representation. It was never going to be easy. But they should draw comfort from the fact that rarely has it been easy anywhere else in the world, even in places supposedly as advanced as the United Kingdom. There, women had to fight for their right for a long time before they eventually got it—and this by the way was not too long ago. Europe and North America gave women the vote a mere few decades ago. So, YES, you will find opposition with some fringe and archaic groups who may continue to hold sway over the moderates, but NO, do not lose hope. There are a lot of men in the Arab world who DO support your cause!

Unfortunately, Arab women cannot win their cause by citing international cases. Rather, they need to find inspiration and knowledge from their own history, society, and religion and win it on their own merit. Fortunately, in the Arab world's history and culture there are plenty of examples of women who have been leaders, businesswomen, teachers, writers, and activists that have done a lot more than most men. More importantly perhaps in Islam, unlike what many may believe, women were emancipated and got rights long before they had elsewhere. Indeed, in the prophet's teachings and in his own behavior, he was a moderate who respected the role that women played, be they in terms of their work, their learning, or their opinion—many a time acquiescing to their demands. And so, Arab women will have to continue building their case based on tenets close to home and particularly close to Islam, joining hands with learned religious scholars who share such beliefs, thus eroding the misuse of Islam by those who oppose them.

The key question to me, though, is what will happen once they do get the vote. For instance, women in Egypt and Lebanon have had the vote for decades, and yet both countries have very little representation in their respective parliaments. Here, I blame the Egyptian and Lebanese women, for letting their own gender down. There is no excuse; for no matter how you slice and dice a voting system, the law of averages will yield 50% of the vote. And so, the question is why have they not voted to be represented by themselves or those who will carry their cause? The answer to this question is typically attributed to several developmental reasons among which is education. But that is no longer the case, as recent UNDP statistics have shown that in most of the Arab world, primary education has been made available to all and in some countries literacy rates for women now EXCEED that of men!

If it is no longer development, could it perhaps simply be political apathy by the female gender?

While some call for quotas, I am actually against quotas, because it might actually hurt the cause of women in the long term; since it might yield "appointed" women parliamentarians who are there at the service of whoever "appointed" them.

Rather, I suggest that Arab women start off focusing on causes that relate to their gender-issues such as healthcare, nutrition, hygiene, education, and family leave—in other words issues that do not often capture the attention or imagination of a great many male parliamentarians. By doing this, first they are able to present themselves as less of a threat to their male counterparts and hence be given more political leeway. Second, it would allow them to better appeal to their gender's vote, thus making sure they get in.

Once in, they should work on getting more and more women in so as to start making a real difference in their respective societies. Only then, may men begin to realize that it was all for a better Arab society.

The great chasm in Lebanese politics (May 2005)

There is a great chasm in Lebanese politics today and it is as wide and as tragic as Don Quixote's chasm with reality. Indeed, Lebanon's political scene sometimes seems to be littered with Quixotian characters, for not only are they battling political windmills, but they are inevitably going to come out as losers.

Take the case of Lebanon's beleaguered Prime Minister Karami. He is about to announce yet another resignation following his two previous ones. The tragedy in this whole matter is that from the day he received his post, Karami never had the political weight nor popularity to carry it. He doesn't have much of a plan, never had one, and even less likelihood to ever have one. For all practical purposes, he is an expired politician who has little sway on the nation's destiny.

As for President Lahoud, it is anyone's guess which national quarter he is getting support from. His legitimacy has been so eroded; few even listen to what he has to say. When he does finally say something, it is torn to pieces with contempt from most of the Lebanese populace. His institutions have failed and so have most of his policies. With Syria's exit, his days are just as numbered as Karami's.

Of course the third member of the so-called troika is non-other than the Speaker of the House, Nabih Berry. Like Lahoud, his support is also evaporating, which is why he has elevated his demands for larger voting district and for proportionate representation—in the hope of squeezing the utmost votes from an ever-disenchanted populace.

If each of the three seem to have Cervantian traits, the three together amount to nothing less than a Quixotian crescendo, which resonates as far from the population's demands and wishes as Quixote's imagination from his comical existence. At a time, when the nation desperately needs to be reunited through an impartial election process, the three politicians cannot even agree on a ministry, whose duties will be temporary until parliamentary elections occur. At a time when millions are marching the streets in Lebanon demanding basic rights, which these leaders do not understand and so simply ignore. At a time when the nation is at the brink of an economic calamity, none has even the slightest clue of a plan, let alone a strategy, or a national vision. Instead of viewing the world around them through the hopeful prism lining Beirut's streets, they see it from a pessimistic existential prism.

As a result, it must be said that the Lebanese people have been overly civil. No government in its right mind "hangs around" with a "let's wait and see" attitude while a third of its population hits the streets protesting. It is not only an affront, it is outright scandalous. Such a government must be deaf, dumb, utterly incompetent, or perhaps a combination of the three. Of course, it could be that there is an orchestrated diversionary tactic to delay the will of the people from occurring through fair election—therefore further widening the political chasm between what the people want and what their government is providing. Whichever the case, the chasm is growing by the day, and such a government simply does not represent the will of the Lebanese people, but rather its own interests. And so, it must be cleansed in all its forms including the presidency, premiership, and parliament.

Some may think that this is a crazy idea, and highly risky. It will create a vacuum, they argue. Such a vacuum already exists, for the constitution, which is supposed to represent the will of the people has been manipulated by a government, which is incapable of meeting the demands of its people. Some fear and warn of chaos, but that is only there because of them. If one million people marched in Lebanon and not a single incident occurred, it is not because of the security apparatus in the country but in spite of it!

The time has come for the Lebanese to chart themselves a fresh new start and eliminate that great political chasm. No "and ifs" or "buts"...

Let Sinyora form a technocratic Cabinet (July 2005)[23]

Once he forms a government—which is itself proving no easy thing—Prime Minister-elect Fouad Sinyora has daunting tasks ahead of him. Not only does he need to address tough economic issues, but he will also need to deal with thorny matters such as President Emile Lahoud's controversial extended mandate, Hezbollah's disarmament, not to mention Lebanese relations with Syria and the international community.

Sinyora is no novice to government. For years he managed one of Lebanon's most difficult portfolios—that of finance. This involved the difficult mission of organizing and reviving Lebanon's post-war finances, including such complex and politically sensitive issues as setting budgets, tax collection, and financing (or refinancing) the national debt. All the while, Sinyora had to cope with a tumultuous political environment. Back then, he was a technocrat doing the bidding of Prime Minister Rafic Hariri, who helped direct and safeguard him in the jungle of Lebanese politics.

---

23   First published by the Daily Star on July 12, 2005.

All this changed when Hariri was assassinated. The resulting political upheaval led to Syria's withdrawal, to the toppling of several security chiefs, and to sweeping parliamentary change—all of which brought the opposition undisputed political power. Hariri himself would have marveled at this new political landscape, had he been alive. Alas, he is not and the assignment of putting this new majority to good use has effectively fallen into Sinyora's lap. No single decision will be as important as the first one he will take, namely forming a government.

All the indications are that Sinyora will be putting together a "political" Cabinet that includes all the main actors in the country. In contrast, Sinyora's predecessor, Najib Mikati, even while he enjoyed a parliamentary majority, chose to form a government made up largely of technocrats. Sinyora should seriously think of making a similar effort, for a number of reasons:

A technocratic government would send a strong signal to the Lebanese people, particularly the young. Following the Syrian withdrawal, Lebanon will have the first freely elected government in some time. This is the moment to send a signal that the old ways are no more and that a new era based on hard, honest and qualified work has dawned. What sort of a moral would the millions of people who marched in protests over the past few months, particularly on March 14, understand if the same old faces showed up yet again in another stalemated Cabinet?

If the core of Sinyora's program—as he outlined in his first speech a few days ago—is the implementation of Ta'ef and the elimination of sectarianism, then what better time to show seriousness in this regard by forming a technocratic government with no direct stake in holding onto power, whose qualifications are undisputable?

A technocratic government may also mean an easier confirmation process, because while Sinyora will please no one in particular in the political class, he will also alienate no one in particular. This could give his Cabinet more immediate leeway, but also down the road will make it easier to take difficult decisions—as Mikati's short-lived government proved on issues as contentious as the election law, the Hariri investigation, and (though final implementation has yet to be confirmed) giving Palestinian refugees in Lebanon a right to work. With a technocratic Cabinet, Sinyora will pursue

113

a clear and cohesive program. That's why his team is much more likely to advance on certain issues than a political Cabinet, whose allegiance and agenda will be set from the outside by powerful stakeholders.

The international community seems ready and willing to help Lebanon, as was reiterated last week by American officials and by French President Jacques Chirac. However, a precondition is for Lebanon to help itself. It would serve Lebanon little to have yet another politically deadlocked government. Better a technocratic one capable of mustering the respect and support of the international community, both of which will be so desperately needed in the months and years ahead.

And last, but perhaps most important, is the fact that Sinyora himself is not a politician, but a technocrat. This means two things: he is likely to work better with other technocrats, and less effectively with politicians.

The time has come for Lebanon's politicians to accept that the country's interests must transcend more parochial political considerations. What better way for the political class to show this than to allow Sinyora to surround himself with a team of apolitical specialists who seek, primarily, to steer Lebanon away from its tragic past and into a bright future?

Lebanon's political system needs revamping not tweaking (August 2005)

Since the infamous popular demonstration of March 14th, much is said to have happened in Lebanon. The Syrians withdrew; elections ushered in a new parliament formed of the opposition, and a new government was formed. The newly elected prime minister proceeded to present an ambitious reform plan.

And yet, notwithstanding all this positive change, early signs have begun to re-emerge of the same old political gridlock that has seemingly plagued every government since Lebanon's independence half a century ago. It started with the typically complex negotiations for the formation of the new cabinet—this in spite of the opposition's unquestionable victory. Since then, however, things have not gotten much better with several newly appointed ministers already threatening to quit because the prime minister tried to kick-off the government's agenda with necessary economic reforms—privatization. On another crucial front—that of security, with bombs exploding every other week and not a single indictment issued to date, there seems to be an impasse on who gets what security post—what is the urgency after all? Similarly, key judicial appointments have been held-off. On the contentious issue of foreign policy and Hezbollah's arms, there seems to be no clear direction on how to approach the UN. Recently, the argument seems to be more focused on who will go to the assembly and not what they will say to allay its stern resolutions.

And so to the dismay of so many hopeful Lebanese, it seems none of the changes and sacrifices that occurred over the past six months have been enough to rid Lebanon of its endemic political stalemate. Has it all been in vain?

Practically, it is difficult to imagine why things would change in a political system built on the false promise of "consensus" and "unity" and indelibly ushering into office cabinets made up of almost every nook and cranny political party in Lebanon. For instance, the current makeup includes leftists, rightists, centrists, conservatives, liberals, socialists, fundamentalists, technocrats, and even intellectuals. Somewhere somehow it seems the objective of Lebanon's governance shifted from tangible execution to "unity". Never mind if it means the primary executive body—that of the council of ministers—ends up with ministers carrying differing ideology and background, varying tactical and strategic political objectives, and whose allegiance is not to the leadership or the cabinet. The important thing, the Lebanese have been sold, is that as long as there is "unity", all else will be fine. And yet empirically, all has not been fine, with some fifty years of undeniable evidence of political instability, civil upheaval, and economic calamity.

The tragedy of it all, of course, is Lebanon's social contract has closed the door on democratic accountability. And so the problem is not "unity", for that is all what Lebanon has had since independence. The problem is not a deficiency of political executives either; Lebanon has had its fair share of highly effective and visionary leaders—not least of which was the late Premier Hariri. Rather, the problem is a political system gridlocked by design, which has proven to be ungovernable, unaccountable, and prone to instability and tampering.

And so, the Lebanese are going to have to make some hard choices going forward: Do they want to be ruled over or do they want to rule themselves? Do they want a truly competitive democratic system; or do they want a sham, which obstinately sidelines the wishes of millions of citizens? Do they want a segregated system, or one which gives all citizens equality and opportunity under the blind eyes of law? Do they want a transparent system, or do they want a system where there are so many preconditions, hardly anyone can decipher let alone be held accountable? Do they want a system based on merit, or do they want a system based on archaic tribalism and clientelism? And finally, do they want a system which unshackles their tremendous global potential, or do they want one curtailing them back ad infinitum?

All this means that tweaking the current political system with this or that election gerrymandering law, as is seemingly being contemplated, is no longer going to cut it. Nothing short of a social contract revamp will do. If this means, eliminating sectarianism, then so be it. If this means unifying executive positions and having direct executive elections, then so be it. If it means having two parliamentary bodies—one permanently sectarian and one not—then so be it. If it means creating secular parties, then so be it. If it means neutralizing Lebanon's foreign policy to disconnect the nation from regional turmoil once and for all, then so be it. If it means institutionalizing Lebanon's resistance, then so be it.

Do the Lebanese have the will to take the brave step of drawing a new social contract commensurate with their new realities, or will they continue to constrain themselves to mediocrity and a highly charged destiny? While the answer to this question remains uncertain, what is certain is that only the Lebanese themselves can answer it, and no one else—not their leaders and not the international community. On March 14th, the Lebanese people showed the world how they took their destiny back into their own hands. It is time they finished the job.

Either case, Lebanese President Lahoud should move on (September 2005)

Defying Lebanese public opinion and the majority in parliament, Lebanese President Emile Lahoud has gone to the United Nation's General Assembly. With many questions lingering back home, his objectives at the UN seem as uncertain as his credibility. What are some of these questions and why are they relevant?

The first one, of course, is whether or not he is guilty of orchestrating Prime Minister Hariri's assassination. Those arguing for the case point to the fact that four generals of the military establishment—some of whom have been close associates of his for decades—have already been jailed and accused of participating in the gruesome murder. 'How is it possible that he did not know about a plot right under his nose to eliminate his own political arch enemy,' people are asking? Lahoud has maintained innocence stating that the UN investigation will prove it by showing who the true culprits are.

While most seem riveted on this question, there is a second less asked but equally important question: If Lahoud is indeed not found to be guilty of the assassination by the UN, is he not in the very least guilty of public mismanagement—particularly the armed and security forces—over which he had been credited with rebuilding and has had reasonable control over? After all, not only did the assassination of Hariri occur under his watch; but so did those of politician George Hawi and journalist Samir Kassir, not to mention the two failed attempts on the lives of Telecom Minister Marwan Hmade and the president's own son-in-law, Defense Minister Elias Murr. If we add to all this the threats that have been received by several politicians in Lebanon forcing them into exile, and some half a dozen or so bombs that have gone off throughout Beirut causing substantial damage to a teetering economy, one begins to see more than just isolated incidents. Rather, what becomes obvious is the complete disintegration of security and order in the nation. Surely, Lahoud cannot deny that these events occurred, nor can he deny his inability to prevent them!

This in itself should be enough to justify his ouster; and the Lebanese need not wait for the international investigation's result to realize that

Lahoud's presidency has expired—regardless of whether he is found guilty of the assassination or not.

Some claim the issue to be more complicated than this, for instance the presidency itself (Maronite interests) would be weakened if Lahoud is forced to step down. Surely, they do not believe that those interests would be furthered if Lahoud stayed on for another two years? In reality the Maronite community and Lebanon at large are hurting because of the current predicament; and the sooner everyone realizes this, the quicker the country as a whole can move on.

Others claim that constitutionally a president may not be forced down. This is quite ironic considering that the whole mess started when the constitution was forcibly amended to extend Lahoud's term. So why not re-amend the constitution and undo the damage? If there is a national will, there is certainly a way.

Others claim that Lahoud is the resistance's first line of defense. Perhaps they are misreading it in that the resistance might be Lahoud's last line of defense. In either case, there is no evidence that the resistance is counting on Lahoud's existence for its own. If it is, then the resistance is indeed much weaker than many people may have perceived it to be. Is it?

And lastly, there are those who have announced that the geopolitical situation has forced Syria and its Lebanese supporters into a corner and that Lahoud's days are numbered anyway. In this, however, they seem to be missing the point, for while it may or may not be true, it does not serve the Lebanese people to leave their presidency's destiny in the hands of outside interests. If anything, the nation's ongoing predicament should have taught the Lebanese this much. Are the Lebanese to repeat the error once more only this time with another president carrying yet another flag with a new set of colors?

For all these questions, President Lahoud is not likely to find answers in the UN, nor will the Lebanese people. The answers and the president's destiny are in Lebanon where they should be, and the only thing that truly matters at this point is whether the common Lebanese person, whatever his or her affiliation, believes that Lahoud continues to be worthy of the presidency and of their aspirations and trust. If not, then their message should be as loud and as clear as that of March 14th: Mr. President, thank you for your service; but regardless of whether you are guilty or not, with all due respect, it is time for you and for Lebanon to move on.

A neutral Lebanon will be a peaceful one (April 2006)[24]

With Lebanon's national dialogue scheduled to resume next week and Hezbollah's arms soon up for discussion, on Wednesday the United Nations envoy Terje Roed-Larsen released his report on the progress of Security Council Resolution 1559. The UN's insistence on full implementation of the resolution risks delegitimizing the government if it does not disarm all groups, including Hezbollah. The party counters that only through arms was it able to force Israel out of Lebanon and that the Lebanese Army has little chance of adequately defending the nation. Instead, Hezbollah's resistance alone can buy Lebanon the security it needs.

Hezbollah's argument is at best incomplete. The party has failed to take into account two key variables besides its ability to enhance external security: domestic stability and international legitimacy, neither of which an armed Hezbollah can offer under existing conditions.

With regards to internal stability, the party's arms have heightened a fear among many Lebanese that, by keeping its weapons, Hezbollah will invite other Lebanese factions that reject Hezbollah's "exceptionalism" to arm themselves. This fear is made more acute by the fact that Lebanon has myriad parties and religious communities supporting different causes, not to mention a large population of Palestinian refugees, many of whom are also armed, living in economic wretchedness. This mix could turn Lebanon into a powder keg, as it was during the 1960s and 1970s.

If Israel decides to withdraw from the Shebaa Farms area, and if the UN continues to insist that the Farms are Syrian, not Lebanese, it will be exceedingly hard for Lebanon to gain the international legitimacy needed to cover for Hezbollah's being armed. This could delegitimize the resistance,

---

24 First published by the Daily Star on April 21, 2006.

something the nation simply cannot afford at a time when it needs all the international support it can get, financial and otherwise.

But even Hezbollah's external security argument is a fundamentally weak one. While the party's weapons have defended Lebanon on occasion in recent years, Israel has not had much of a reason to reinvade Lebanon since withdrawing its soldiers in May 2000. If, however, Hezbollah proves to be too much of a threat, this could well lead to another Israeli invasion, as happened in 1982 to expel the Palestinian Liberation Organization. Hezbollah's military prowess may end up not deterring Israel, but actually encouraging it to again resort to violence.

With this in mind, how can Lebanon overcome this dilemma? What "strategic security" option is there allowing it to advance internal stability, international legitimacy, and external security, without provoking a confrontation with Hezbollah or the international community? The answer may be simpler than many realize: neutrality enshrined in the Constitution. While not a new idea, neutrality's time may have finally come.

Neutrality is defined as "non-participation in armed conflicts with other states," and it is a status recognized in international law (namely in the Hague agreements of 1907). Neutrality is declared by a state, but also has to be accepted by key players in the international community.

Why is it timely for Lebanon? Because it meets the three aforementioned prerequisites for strategic security. First, it would buttress internal stability by eliminating the justification for factions to be armed in order to protect themselves. It would also eliminate the divisiveness that ensues when groups or communities side with or allow themselves to be manipulated by outside powers. The only side all Lebanese factions would constitutionally be allowed to take is that of defending neutrality.

Second, from an international legitimacy perspective, Lebanon would avoid the thorny issue of signing peace deals, namely with Israel, while benefiting from the international protective umbrella of neutrality. Even if Israel withdraws from the Shebaa area, therefore, peace discussions could be put off until the Arab-Israeli conflict is resolved.

Third, and notwithstanding its constitutional neutrality and international protection, Lebanon could continue to have both an active army and a trained and ready resistance (which would need to be funded by the state and be open to all Lebanese) to protect its external security. Nevertheless, because of Lebanese neutrality the message to external countries would be loud and clear: this force is uniquely designed for defensive purposes.

As Lebanon prepares to fully regain control over its destiny, strategic security, as Hezbollah officials have pointed out, is indeed a crucial issue. Constitutionally guaranteed neutrality, approved by the international community and backed by a defensive army and resistance, is a solution offering internal stability, international legitimacy, and external security. Is this not what all Lebanese and the international community want?

A Plan Colombia for Lebanon? (August 2006)

As the Lebanon donor conference in Sweden is being prepared, many in the international community are beginning to ask about the type and amount of help needed. Some are trying on the cheap, others clinging to some reconstruction "catchphrase" models such as the Marshal Plan or even the Iraqi Plan—which by most counts are overly ambitious. Perhaps Lebanon's needs may be more in line with those of Colombia, under what has become famously known as Plan Colombia.

Over the past few years, similarities between Lebanon and Colombia have become uncanny. Like its South American counterpart, Lebanon enjoys one of the oldest democracies in its direct neighborhood. Unfortunately, just like Colombia, Lebanon suffers from unrelenting violence, which threatens this democracy; for like Colombia's FARC, Hezbollah is an armed and belligerent group which while enjoying support from a portion of the local population is branded terrorist by the international community—primarily the United States. Even though arguably Hezbollah is not nationally outlawed as the FARC is, it acts independently of the Lebanese government, receives outside support from ominous sources, and is currently acting against international law—namely UN resolutions 1559 and 1701.

While Lebanon faces many uncertainties, the recent war has highlighted two certainties. First, Lebanon's democracy is in jeopardy; and second, Lebanon needs as much international support as it can get if it is to stay as a viable state. It is precisely here where Lebanon can learn from Colombia's experience with Plan Colombia, and where particularly the United States can step up and lend its support—as it did for the government of Colombia—in the process assuring its own long term regional interests.

According to the US State Department, Plan Colombia is an "integrated strategy to meet the most pressing challenges confronting Colombia"— including promoting the peace process, disarming the belligerent groups, reviving the Colombian economy, and strengthening the democratic pillars of Colombian society. As eerie as it may sound, Plan Colombia also included strengthening Colombia's army and sending it to the south of the country where guerilla groups had taken over in a quasi-state within a state scheme. In addition though, Plan Colombia included alternative economic development as well as support for displaced persons due to the conflict.

Launched in 1999 as a 5-Year plan, Plan Colombia's total funding was US$7.5 billion. The US support to Plan Colombia started at US$330 million with an initial total commitment of US$1.3 billion. As execution and positive results became apparent, this was ultimately raised to a total of US$2 billion. The balance was funded by Colombia itself as well as other international donors. The results have been stark. In 5 Years, Colombia transformed itself into becoming its region's stalwart, its military asserted itself nationally rendering the guerillas irrelevant, paramilitary groups rejoined society's mainstream, peace and stability was retained, and the national economy is now booming. Plan Colombia is by all means a success story to be emulated.

While Lebanon is indeed a smaller nation than Colombia, the magnitude of its problems in the aftermath of the Israeli attacks is in no way smaller. The economic damage of the recent war is still being assessed, but most analysts seem to be pointing to US$5 billion in damages, including livelihood, infrastructure, and property damage. This figure, however, does not include the cost of beefing up Lebanon's military, which should be seen as a key tenet moving forward.

Of course, some may express execution concerns. In Fouad Sinyora, though, Lebanon provides technocratic abilities having been finance minister under Prime Minister Rafic Hariri's governments and reconstructed most of the government's fiscal finances, tax collection, customs, among other key institutions. He could be entrusted to execute and fulfill his government's obligations.

For this to happen, however, Prime Minister Sinyora and his government need all the international support they can get. Coming up with a Plan Colombia for Lebanon is a crucial first step. The United States administration has got to step up and play a key role in the process. While realizing that there is Iraq "fatigue" in the administration, now is no time to shy away from the fine goal of turning Lebanon around once and for all. Taking the successful case of Plan Colombia and applying it to Lebanon could be the right way. Substantial financial aid aimed at beefing up Lebanon's national military and economy will not only render those against such plans irrelevant, but it is also likely to rejuvenate American and international hopes of a democratically stable, peaceful, and prosperous Middle East.

Lebanon must prevail and it will (August 2006)

As the Lebanese sift through the rubble, bury the dead, and assess the massive extent of damage to the nation, many in Lebanon see the situation as bleak; others see it as hopeless. "The war has taken Lebanon back decades," some say, while others have simply packed and left altogether. And yet, while the war was arguably the result of many miscalculations, for the Lebanese and the world at large to write-off Lebanon would be an even bigger mistake. Lebanon is much more than what has been lost.

To begin with, Lebanon remains an invaluable social experiment tried in few places around the world. The persistent religious coexistence of Christians and Muslims in Lebanon, as the late Pope John Paul II once expressed, is a "message to the world". It is an affront to those preaching clash of civilizations. No better has this been exemplified than in the recent opening of doors of most regions and religions in Lebanon to refugees from Lebanon's destroyed areas—regardless of denomination. Israeli bombs managed to prove what many naysayers refused to believe. Indeed if anything, it proved that Lebanon remains a lot more religiously open and accommodating than Israel proper.

Lebanon also remains a political entity rarely attempted in the rest of the Arab World. Its democracy is still standing even after sixty years of calamities. While Lebanon's democracy can be improved, if ever there was a doubt of democracy's potential entrenchment in the Arab world, Lebanon proves otherwise; for it has survived numerous wars, invasions, and political assassinations. In a sea of powerful autocracies and dictatorships, Lebanon's democratic model—not so long ago showcased by the "Cedar Revolution"—stands firmly and obstinately.

Lebanon's government back on its feet for more than a decade is intact and has proven itself capable and willing to deal with the massive challenges being presented. Prime Minister Sinyora's government has not only withstood massive pressures, but managed to convert itself into a proactive catalyst presenting practical solutions that would allow Lebanon to inch towards lasting peace and stability. Its recent bold move offering to send the Lebanese army to the South highlighted its ability to build a national consensus allowing Lebanon to take its destiny into its own hands. By doing so, the Lebanese government also managed to disarm its opponents by getting solid endorsement from the Arab League as well as the United Nations.

Militarily, the Lebanese resistance's stance now ranks as second to none in facing up to the powerful Israeli army. The military stalemate has shown both the Lebanese and the Israelis that war will be extremely costly to both sides with no clear victory possible. Ironically, this has the potential of creating a de facto stability if Lebanon's resistance agrees to avoid confronting the international community and join its rank and file to Lebanon's army.

And finally, Lebanon as an economy is also much more than the destruction inflicted by Israel. Economies are not built or destroyed in a day or a month. They are built over years and decades one step at a time. Sure Lebanon's economy will suffer in the short term, but Lebanese tenacity, entrepreneurship, competitiveness, and innovation all remain—no matter how many Israeli bombs have fallen. Lebanon's economy will rise again, one worker at a time, one business at a time, and one industry at a time.

While the Lebanese should be on their guard, they should be patient and should not despair. Lebanon's ideals must prevail; and hopefully they will.

Islam & Islamists: A threat or an echo (September 2006)

Brushstroke West versus Islam theories resulting in these false associations affected policy. Policy led to action against some of these groups, which only stoked the brewing discontent and fed into their more fundamental elements. In Lebanon, for instance, one year after the peaceful Cedar revolution, Israel, which prides itself for it "anti-terrorist" struggle saw itself once more facing-off with its arch nemesis Hezbollah in the 2006 Second Lebanon War. The Israeli objective at the outset of the war was the liberation of two abducted soldiers. Hezbollah countered by stating that these soldiers are its way of liberating Lebanese held in Israeli prisons. Nonetheless, Israel decided to launch an all-out war, and by the end of it, the objective had changed to wiping out the group. The basic assumption, of course, was that the group was a terrorist militia, which would not stand up and fight against the Israeli might. If anyone should have known better, it was Israel because they had been facing off with this group since the early 1990's. Another assumption was that by bombing civilian Lebanese infrastructure, the people would be driven to turn against the group. As it turns out, both of these assumptions proved wrong. The group held its ground for a month sometimes in areas less than 1 kilometer from the Israeli border. The Lebanese people who had been wary of Hezbollah began viewing Israeli actions as excessive, and they began supporting the group. Israel's subsequent failure to meet any of its objectives seems to have done nothing other than embolden the group. According to Israeli journalists Harel and Issacharoff, who wrote a book about this specific conflict, "Israel became the main reason for Hezbollah's prosperity."[25]

By using these over-simplified theories to apply policy, some Western policy makers began grouping Islam, political Islam, and militant Islam in one uniform basket. The resulting solutions hence applied were dogmatically over-simplistic and proved to be strategically detrimental. This tended to deepen the negative regional perceptions and resentments. At a time when US state department initiatives such as MEPI (Middle East Partnership

---

25 Harel, Amos and Issacharoff, Avi, *34 Days Israel, Hezbollah, and the War in Lebanon*, Palgrave MacMillan, 2008, pg. 21.

Initiative) were being launched to win the hearts and minds of Arabs, their policies spoke otherwise. In an interesting conversation I had with the president of an American non-profit organization operating in Lebanon, he states that his mission was to train elementary school teachers around the country. And yet he lamented the difficulty it was proving to get funding from USAID because of fears that some of this training might be deployed in schools in areas where Hezbollah operates. Ironically, he stated these are the areas where his organization was most needed and would make most difference. This policy, he told me, had "no heart, nor mind".

The irony does not stop there. As opposed to such generalizations and all sweeping rejection of anything to do with Islam, more microanalysis and intricate policies are needed. For instance, in Arab countries where the vast majority is indeed Muslim, it does not only manifest itself through the extreme. It has many divisions and manifestations that are the natural growth of a developing society. In fact, it is not much different than many Western countries, the United States included. In his insightful book on America's democracy titled *Hamilton's Republic*, Michael Lind, alludes to similar divisions in America,

"Religion, like race, should not be confused with ethnicity. Like race in America, religion in America tends to be much more permanent and stable than ethnicity. The pattern in the US has been that immigrant churches become de-ethnicized or Americanized after only a few generations...The post ethnic American religion or denomination may continue to be divided, but it will be divided along theological or political lines (the North-South division among denominations like the Methodists and Baptists originated from political disputes over slavery). Thus differences among Polish, German, and Russian Jews have been replaced by division among Reform, Conservative, and Orthodox Jews in America...The American nation has always been divided by race and religion and will continue to be divided

along religious lines even if race fades away as a concept; but those are divisions within a nation, not between nations."[26]

If in a nation as relatively democratic as the United States, religion is seen as a root, and one around which nuanced ideologies have emerged, why should we oppose or expect a dissimilar sort of development in a democratizing Arab world?

Ironically, it is but an echo of what happened in the West; for Christian autocrats were just as reluctant in giving up their power to the masses as their modern-day Arab counterparts. Watson and Barber give interesting insight:

After the fall of Athens, the Greek idea of democracy all but disappeared for nearly two thousand years. The idea of law persisted, however, while the fresh notion of Christian brotherhood that spread during the Roman period helped to preserve the ideal of equality. Together the two kept alive the crucial Athenian concept of insonomia (equality before the law) following the fall of Rome, right through the Renaissance. But the outrageous idea that the people of a nation rule themselves had little currency in the Roman and Renaissance worlds and where it did appear in Europe, it often seemed more a threat than a promise... To property owners, monarchs, and rulers, democracy- the idea that all people could participate in the affairs of government- seemed to advance the notion that the rabble could rule: government by the ignorant many and the envious poor.[27]

---

26 Lind, Michael, *Hamilton's Republic*, The Free Press, 1997, pg. 44-46.
27 Watson, Patrick and Barber, Benjamin, *The Struggle for Democracy*, Democracy Films Ltd., 1988, pg. 29.

Israeli fear and the pain it inflicts (January 2008)

The other day on the radio, I heard something startling. As a result of Israel's incursion into Palestine, 5 Israelis had been killed and some 500 Palestinians too—among whom are women, children, and in some cases entire families. Unfortunately, this wasn't the surprising part, for over the years we have gotten used to these lopsided Israeli war results. The truly amazing thing was an Israeli minister being interviewed who stated that this was "Israel's response to constantly living in fear". Interesting argument, to say the least, but let me understand this straight: Israel, supposedly the shining beacon in the Middle East, is 'afraid' even when it can inflict 100/1 losses on its enemies? This didn't make much sense to me and it resulted in a nagging question: "What is Israel really afraid of?" I began asking around.

One person explained, "The Israelis have to uproot the Islamic terrorist element from their surroundings, because they are an existential threat." Compelling argument, and yet if anything, Israel's actions since its invasion of Lebanon back in 1982 have done the exact opposite. While it did manage to expel the PLO (who are actually nationally secular in nature) from Lebanon during that invasion, its actions helped create alternatives such as Hezbollah (more Islamic), which has proven to be a far more difficult adversary. In fact, Hezbollah is now recognized to have expelled Israel proper out of Lebanon in 2000, released most of the Lebanese prisoners in Israeli jails in 2004 and 2008, and even beat Israel in the 2006 war as attested to by Israeli and American military and intelligence reports.

Another answered, "Israel is trying to exterminate the Palestinians because they live under the weight of an unviable Jewish national concept, which cloaks the injustice being imposed on the Palestinians with the past tragedies befallen the Jews—a weight so heavy that it threatens Israel itself as a national concept." Another interesting argument leading us to a sort of qualitative human tragedy balance of sorts. In other words, those whose misery can be sold more effectively to the world could emerge victors. After all, as tragic as it may seem, over the past 60 years, it seems the Israelis have done a much better job selling their holocaust misery and its injustice to such a degree that their own massacres in Lebanon and Palestine have become qualitatively irrelevant to the world. Through their action, have Israelis implicitly convinced the world that the blood and flesh of some carry less weight than others?

Yet another stated, "If the Israelis are not in a constant state of war justifying their own national struggle for existence, they fear they will cease to exist as a nation." So, essentially, Israel is not the Athens that many say the West implanted to lead the Middle East out of its 'dark ages', but rather nothing more than a modern day version of Sparta—a military parasite state feeding off those around it, and particularly the weak. If that were so, would it not mean that its end could eventually meet the same implosive and bloody end as Sparta's?

And finally, one confidently informed me that waging these senseless wars coupled with the now customary out-of-the-box media blitz (using the same Israeli TV talking heads) is Israel's only way of making sure it continues to receive the billions in military support from the US and others. Interesting point, although I am not sure American politicians need much convincing to give or extend Israel any funding. In the US, when it comes to Israel, a blank military check seems to be Standard Operating Procedure regardless of the fact that Israel is said to already have enough arsenal to zap the entire region back to the Stone Age many times over.

So we come back to the question of fear: What is it that Israel is afraid of? Are any of its fears truly justified, or is it possible that Israel's fear has reached a point where it is feeding on itself and in the process warped itself into some self-fulfilling nightmare? And if so, have we as humans not seen enough atrocities justified by fear-mongering in the course of history (including the Holocaust) to reach a point where we say enough is enough? Apparently not yet. In the meantime, scores of Palestinians continue to feel the pain, inflicted by Israeli fears.

Saad Hariri and the outlook of a new generation (July 2009)

As the new cabinet begins to take shape under Lebanon's new Prime Minister, Saad Hariri, questions abound as to which direction he is going to take and what he will focus on. Some believe he will simply be a continuation of the predecessor governments with his hands bound to much of the same politics. After all, the March 14th coalition has been in power since 2005, and recent polls only served to reaffirm its position. They conclude that everything is likely to remain the same. This reading, however, is incomplete in that it disregards two key factors: First the changing geopolitical setting and second and perhaps more importantly Saad Hariri himself.

With respect to the geopolitical setting, in which the emerging prime minister finds himself, one is inclined to say it is positive—and much more favorable than that faced by his father, the late Prime Minister Rafic Hariri and his successor, Prime Minister Fouad Sinyora. Internationally, under the Obama administration, the US is likely to be much less confrontational and a lot more accommodating—particularly with regards to Iran—as was recently the case with its hands-off policy to that country's controversial election results and the subsequent opposition crackdown.

This development could be coupled with the regional Saudi-Syrian rapprochement that has seen Syria opening normal diplomatic ties with Lebanon and its foreign minister even signaling border demarcation. Syria seems to be growing more comfortable with Lebanon's kaleidoscopic defensive arrangement of UNIFIL forces, a strengthening Lebanese army, and an untouchable Hezbollah resistance. Recent massive Israeli military maneuvers in the South, which in the past could have caused a major stir, seem to have had little reaction beyond rhetoric, and an Israeli war on Lebanon has never been as unlikely. In parallel, the potentially divisive issue of the International court, tasked with prosecuting those behind the assassination of Prime Minister Rafic Hariri also seems to be well on its way and out of the hands of any party within or outside of Lebanon. All this indicates that Lebanon and its incoming prime minister have been given some respite from all the geopolitical crises faced by previous governments, and for a change may be able to proactively govern.

And so the question becomes, how will Saad Hariri govern? Judging by the above-mentioned geopolitical developments, it seems the only place he can proactively focus on and attempt to leave a mark is likely to be the economy. The fact that his business education and work experience are complementary to such a focus are encouraging, but he will need to take full advantage of the current positive economic conditions and place much of his team's efforts on moving the country forward in innovative ways so as to avoid old stalemates.

His team will need to rethink Lebanon's economic development and find new and original ways to engage with regions and social strata that are in most need of it. They will need to jumpstart employment by finding and generating jobs for the Lebanese inside and outside of Lebanon. Establishing private public partnerships to alleviate poverty is a key to regaining the trust in government of a large portion of disenfranchised citizens. Education leading to tangible productivity increases and work opportunities should be pushed. Introducing technology into different aspects of society through ICT initiatives and readiness would yield economic advantages. Foreign assistance, partnerships, and grants should be sought with vibrancy, with knowledge transfer to Lebanon as a requirement. While fiscal austerity measures aimed at stabilizing the national debt should continue, transparent metrics should be created to measure and monitor performance, which should be shared with the general populace instilling modern governance practices that aim to establish trust and encourage society to get involved.

It is understandable if skeptics might call all this wishful thinking. But they must not forget that Saad Hariri is young and belongs to a new generation, which is educated, well-informed, inter-connected with the world, and well-travelled. His generation is the Internet generation, which can see the rest of world at work. It is a generation, which could seek to apply change to old ways so as to elevate the nation's standings. But it is also the very same generation, which in its childhood was the first to taste the bitterness of disastrous policies leading to war. And so it must now choose, whether to leave its own children with a better nation, one which is economically just, prosperous, and open to all its citizens regardless of class, religion, or creed; or alternatively to leave it's children with yet another catastrophe.

Prime Minister Saad Hariri may owe where he is to his father. Where he goes from here and how history and his fellow Lebanese citizens will judge him depends to a large degree on his actions, policy choices, and perhaps his ability to motivate his fellow countrymen and women to rise to the occasion.

What Lebanon's youth needs (March 2010)

The Nature of the Problem: The youth in Lebanon are disenfranchised. Education and illiteracy rates are stagnant, there is little conditioning or value given to excellence, and mediocrity rules in sports and other activities at a time when smaller nations have risen up on a global level. Adding insult to injury, Lebanon's youth does not have a voice to channel its grievances and frustrations. By the time the youth get to voting age, a large percentage is either negatively conditioned or has migrated abroad seeking livelihood.

Some potential strategies and solutions: There is no silver bullet to solve the problem of Lebanon's youth. Rather, there needs to be a proactive, concerted, and sustained effort with clear strategies on five identified fronts.

First, Education: Lebanon's youth needs to be fully educated and prepared to the upcoming challenges this century. Education is one of the keys to the future of Lebanon's youth, and to Lebanon itself. Lebanon's goal should be 100% basic education rates by 2020 with illiteracy completely eradicated. Laws need to be enacted and strictly enforced in this regard. Any parents unwilling to send their children to basic schooling should be held accountable. There is no future or hope without literacy, and there is no excuse for society not to give a vulnerable child every chance possible to acquire a basic education. Once this is accomplished, there needs to be a move to the next goal—by 2030 to provide 100% high school graduation rates with science, math, business, economics, and language arts capabilities—all of which will be direly needed for the nation to be able to compete this century. By 2040, the goal should be to move universality in the direction of colleges—for which the establishment of a network of community colleges may become a necessity. These are aggressive goals, for sure, but if Lebanon hopes to thrive in the future it will need to aggressively educate ALL its sons and daughters WITHOUT EXCEPTION and certainly not based on religion or creed. Education is the first step that needs to be taken on the long road to sustained social and economic prosperity.

Second, Conditioning Objective Excellence: A young person who sees others advance unfairly will be negatively conditioned. Negative conditioning eventually yields disrespect of the law and the rules. It is not what I do that becomes my measure, but rather the son of whom I am, which is an attitude that destroys the youth's hopes and values very early on. In a world that is bound to compete for human resources, this negative conditioning will be the major factor behind brain drain, as those treated unfairly in some societies will seek societies that appreciate and value their talents. Therefore, the key principal should be advancements based on actions and results. Strategically, one and only one measure for advancement should be taken and that is objective excellence. Those that do improvements or aim at excellence need to be rewarded. For this to happen, a strategy needs to permeate from the top-down to objectively condition youth on the merits of excellence. Equally important, those judging the merit and the metrics behind them need to be held accountable. Lebanon's youth needs to be able to build itself on its own objective merits. It is the obligation of the preceding generations to provide Lebanon's youth with measuring sticks and that they be fair and objective. Exact quantitative goals need to be set and performance measured.

Third, Competitiveness & Sports: No one really knows how good they are in anything before they benchmark themselves against others. This applies at a micro as well as macro level. It is the way the world works. Lebanon needs to embrace the spirit of national competitiveness in all its aspects. This starts at early age. At a young age, kids need to be entered into scholastic as well as sports, and other activity competitions. This could start local, but could turn national, regional, and international. Sports in particular need to be pushed at all levels and for both genders. For this to happen, it is imperative that parents be taught how to support their kids. A national strategy to educate parents to stand behind their youth is key as behind every champion is a family that sacrificed to get this champion to the finish line. The youth will not be able to do it alone. Marketing success needs to be pursued too; and athletes and teams need to be promoted to national hero status pretty much like everywhere else. This may be as much a private initiative as it is a national one.

Fourth, Globalization & Opportunities: Lebanon is a speck on the global map. The people who have inhabited this speck over the previous three millennia have all known that to survive and thrive means looking to the outside world. Counter-intuitively, if Lebanon hopes to keep its youth, it cannot do so by restricting their exit, but rather embracing global opportunities that can benefit them and Lebanon. The Phoenicians realized this 3,000 years ago, and the area of current Lebanon thrived under their global expansion. This is a message that escapes many current leaders, who only see the negative aspects of globalization and the migration it is leading to. Indeed, globalization could be a threat if one does nothing about it, but if it is embraced and harnessed, it could be the source of great national wealth. Practically, a strategy that aims to bring closer the diaspora with Lebanon's youth needs to be employed. It should allow Lebanese businesses or organizations led by Lebanese leaders throughout the world to tap into the country's youth and provide them with apprenticeship and travel opportunities. The youth in Lebanon needs to experience and breathe the world. It will give Lebanon's youth a global perspective that will prepare them for the future of a world with quickly dissipating boundaries, but it will also teach them to appreciate their nation more and work on improving it where it needs improvement. It will also open the eyes of the diaspora to invest in Lebanon as they begin to see the benefits of hiring Lebanese youth, which could be a stepping stone from insourcing to outsourcing, keeping or creating high paying jobs in Lebanon. This cannot happen overnight as there are many trust barriers and business idiosyncrasies that will need to be broken down. But with the right strategy and execution, it can be done.

Fifth, Participation: Last but certainly not least, the youth needs their voice to be heard. They currently form a large portion of the population. If Lebanon desires to maintain a working democracy, it will need to bring in as much of its population into the democratic process and as soon as possible. The youth needs to express itself, experiment, and find its own truths and paths. Leaders should be brave in allowing the youth—independent of creed or religion—to participate, and the meaningless argument of sectarian imbalances at 18 needs to be dropped; for it will remain the same when they reach 21. Actually, the more the youth is held back, the more of a national backlash there may be. Giving the youth a voice, will allow the country to listen and understand what they need and want. It will allow them to mature earlier and take responsibility of their democratic choices. Perhaps most importantly, it will allow the isolated youth groups not to grow frustrated at one another, but rather learn to communicate early in a more inclusive democratic process. The youth brings new ideas that need to be heard if Lebanon is going to extract itself from the vicious cycle it has been in since independence.

The Lebanese government is dead, Long live the Lebanese government (January 2011)

Lebanon's government died yesterday after eleven ministers quit from a rather precarious coalition. It transpired a mere 14 months after its inception. Many have started calling for doomsday scenarios forgetting that since Lebanon's independence in 1943, the average government has averaged around 16 months. This government was never going to be an exception. In fact, it may just as well go down in history as being one with among the fewest tangible accomplishments. So the stage is now set for the next act in the Lebanese political drama and that is to choose the next prime minister and government. Some are already claiming that the deposed Prime Minister, Saad Hariri, can be the only choice and they cite three primary reasons. First, they claim he enjoys the majority of the Sunni vote; second, that there is no other candidate with his capabilities; and third, that no candidate will dare oppose his father, Rafic Hariri's international tribunal because it would lead to a Sunni humiliation.

The first claim that Hariri represents the majority of the Sunni vote is the least convincing. While enjoying the support of a community is certainly a plus, it has never been necessary or sufficient for an appointment. His father, Prime Minister Rafic Hariri, lost the premiership in 1998 to Salim Hoss and to Karamu in 2004 even though he enjoyed the majority of Sunni support in both cases. In fact, recent Lebanese Prime Ministers such as Mikati, Karami, Hoss, and Wazzan never had Sunni majorities and yet all became prime ministers. And if some were to argue that this was due to Syrian tutelage, as recently as 2008, the case of General Michel Aoun's failed run for the Lebanese Presidency became the quintessential example of the precariousness of sectarian majority when running for national office. Aoun who had led the anti-Syrian Christian movement while in exile, enjoyed the

135

Maronite Christian majority vote upon his return to Lebanon; and yet Aoun could never translate it into a presidential term. Ironically, then member of parliament Saad Hariri himself led the opposition against Aoun arguing that the Lebanese constitution calls for reconciliatory candidates, who could maintain the national accord. Aoun finally bowed to the pressure (even though by then fully supported by Syria and its Lebanese allies). General Michel Suleiman—also a Maronite and military establishment man, but one who had neither been in politics nor had any political party around him as Aoun did—was elected President. It would seem rather hypocritical for some to come now and claim that having the majority of a sect should automatically mean appointment.

The second claim aims to highlight Prime Minister Saad Hariri's incomparable international credentials and capabilities. While there is no question that he inherited his father's wealth and contact list, the question is whether this is what Lebanon needs at this juncture. The symbolic timing of the eleven ministers' resignation as Hariri was meeting in Washington, DC with US President Obama (having met French President Sarkozy and Saudi King Abdullah shortly before) was lost on no-one. The opposition was unequivocally sending a message to Hariri that Lebanon's solution is not in Washington, France, or Riyadh but in his own Beirut backyard.

While one has to be sympathetic to the prime minister's predicament—it is his father's murder tribunal after all—the harsh reality is that with or without it the nation is still in dire need of a functioning government. Lebanon should not expect to derive wellbeing from knowing who killed Rafic Hariri any more than it does knowing when Israel plans to attack next, but rather from micro-policies managing the affairs of its citizens, helping them find work, and educating their children. Those arguing for a direct correlation will find it difficult to explain Lebanon's economic performance lately. The prime minister's contentious tenure tells the tale of a man weighed down by a difficult conflict of interest. Unfortunately, it is equally hard to imagine how this will change if he returns.

This leads us to the third claim and it is that any other Sunni candidate opposed to the tribunal is bound to face the wrath of a humiliated Sunni community. Firstly, this assumes that the Lebanese Sunni community has not been humiliated in the past when in fact it has seen its fair share of assassinated prime ministers including its first, Riad el Solh, its most appointed, Rashid Karami, and of course it's most celebrated, Rafic Hariri—not mentioning assassinated grand muftis. Implicitly though, does this argument not assume that these assassinations are the only form of humiliation Lebanese Sunnis are currently facing? Simply walking the streets of cities such as Tripoli and Saida (both of which are predominantly Sunni) not to mention some Sunni areas within Beirut shows accentuating dilapidation within the community. Some Sunnis may indeed be livid, but the fundamental source of their frustration is not those opposing the tribunal, but rather the dwindling conditions they find themselves in.

The next prime minister needs to accept this reality and balance their fears and demands with those of other Lebanese communities—something which the outgoing prime minister unfortunately has been unable to do.

The Lebanese Government is Dead ... Long Live the Lebanese Government!

Section Four:
Arab Spring
(2011-2012)

SECTION FOUR:
ARAB SPRING
(2011-2012)

O ver the previous decade, I had the good fortune to travel extensively throughout the Arab world and talk with many young Arabs. Numerous visits to different countries would give me insight into the massive changes occurring. Visiting Arab nations from the Mashreq in the East all the way to the Maghreb in the West affirmed much of what my research was suggesting—change was everywhere. It was affecting the three sub-regions: the Gulf countries, the Levant states, as well as their North African brethren. The fact that all these nations were increasingly interconnected meant that the traditional barriers impeding change would sooner or later come hurtling down.

Perhaps no more was change as marked as in the Arab Gulf countries. The United Arab Emirates, which I began visiting as a kid in the 1970's had begun a serious development project in the mid-1990's. By 2005, Dubai had turned itself into a world class city with highways, hotels, conference centers, skyscrapers, and a massive airport that connected its flights from places as far as New Zealand and São Paulo in Brazil. Soon satellite cities targeting certain sectors began propping up all around the city of Dubai. The first was the Dubai Internet City, which I went often to for work purposes. Soon it was followed by Media City. This thematic-city model would prove to be so successful that Knowledge City, Financial city, Sports City, Health Care City ... among others mushroomed.

Equally interesting to me were the effects Dubai's growth was having on neighboring cities and countries. Abu Dhabi seeing what its sister Emirate was doing, and endowed with the lion's share of the country's oil reserves, decided to draft its own plans. I came across some of these plans projecting the nation forward by several decades. The plans were as elaborate as they

141

were ambitious—taking everything into account from population growth patterns, to wealth distribution, to environmental impact. These plans soon saw a transformation from paper to real world projects. Granted some projects left one bewildered by excessive extravagance, the fact that they were carried through to completion to some was a welcomed regional novelty regardless of sense or merit. This development bug and desire for improvement would soon prove to be infectious. Qatar, which is as endowed as the UAE but with natural gas, soon decided to push its own development plan. Saudi Arabia soon followed suit with plans to build its own industrial cities of a magnitude yet to be seen. Bahrain wanting to protect its own regional role as a financial center soon declared its own plans and added to it the marketing allure of becoming a Formula 1 racing destination. In Bahrain, however, I would come across an interesting regional anomaly.

I travelled to Bahrain in 2006. While it was a very short flight from neighboring Qatar, I quickly learned that unlike its Gulf neighbor, Bahrain did not have much oil or gas, but rather has depended for much of its history (past and modern) on trade and banking. It had done fairly well, but for some reason, did not seem to be as dynamic as either Qatar or the UAE. I did not understand why at first, and attributed it mainly to its lack of hydrocarbon resources. Then one day riding a local cab in the capital Manama, I found the answer staring me in the face. The driver appeared in his sixties and was dressed in a traditional abaya.[28] I found this a little odd, as anyone who has travelled to this part of the world knows that basic labor is usually imported from Central and South Asia. Intrigued, I asked the man in English where he was from. He apologized that he didn't speak any English. From his accent, I knew he spoke Arabic; so I struck up a conversation with the man. Somewhat reticent at first, he opened up to me, when he realized I was Lebanese. He said he was a proud father who had raised several kids but that he had been

---

28 Abaya is the traditional Arab dress that men wear. In Saudi Arabia it is typically white with a checkered-red cover for the head. In the UAE it is white with white head cover. In some other countries in the Gulf it may be more colorful. Sometimes the color may imply social rank. The Bahraini cab driver wore it charcoal with no head scarf.

working as a cab driver for most of his life because of his limited education, difficulties in finding employment, and the lack of growth opportunities. When I asked him why this was the case when there appeared to be so much reform, development, and construction around in Bahrain, his answer was simply, "All this talk of reform is not real. Opportunities are not open to my kind of Bahraini citizen. You see I am Shiite!" I was startled to hear it and must say a bit taken aback. At a time, when millions of foreign laborers were being imported to do work in the Gulf, I found it inexplicable that some portions of the Bahraini population were being left out for whatever reason, let alone sectarianism. It was disconcerting to say the least; and as a Lebanese who had lived through the implications of such short-sighted policies, I knew fully well that it did not bode well on the future of Bahrain. Several years later, it would come as no surprise to me when some of those disenfranchised Bahrainis rose up against their state.

Other parts of the Arab world were also beginning to witness dramatic change. One surprise was to see how much the region had become interconnected. One could see in plain sight—as I had in Damascus, Amman, and Riyadh—satellite dishes lined up across the skyline. Arab satellite was connecting everyone. When meeting Arabs in different parts, everyone seemed to know what was going on in places such as Beirut, Cairo, and Dubai. Information for all intent and purposes was free flowing—even more so in Egypt. I remember upon arriving to Cairo in 2005, I enquired about the availability of the Internet. Immediately I was asked if I wanted "paid or the free" Internet. Curious, as I had never been asked this question in any of my travels, I asked for the difference between one and the other. The answer took me by a bit by surprise, "Sir, here in Egypt dial-up Internet is free for the entire population. But for quicker bandwidth, you would have to pay". I decided to start off with the free service; and found it worked quite well! I guess millions of others in Egypt were also beginning to jump heavily on the Internet—all part of the reform that the Egyptian government had embarked upon around that time. Information and Communication Technology (ICT) investments were in vogue in the region with places like Morocco and Egypt eager to position themselves as service centers for much larger IT consuming nations.

Around that time, on a flight I took from Dubai to Casablanca, I remember being first surprised at the vast expanse below. The trip traversing the Arab world from East to West is a whopping 8 hours—almost the same as crossing the Russian or Canadian expanse and almost double that of the continental United States. Unlike the American continent where a trip say from North Carolina to California does not alter much in terms of the visibility of governance, arriving in the famous Moroccan city, I could not help but notice dilapidated streets, uncollected garbage piles, and poverty indicators everywhere. This stood in stark contrast to the highways and orderliness of the Gulf Emirate I had left a few hours earlier. How long would people in parts of the region accept mismanagement when seeing their Arab brethren elsewhere off to the global races? While economic policies such as pushing ICT were good, these societies were not going to turn into Silicon Valley overnight. There were more pressing issues they needed to work on. Poverty and unemployment were still rampant. Illiteracy was still high (Morocco has one of the lowest literacy rates in the Arab World). Roads needed maintenance. Garbage needed collection. With what appeared like burgeoning populations, it seemed like these countries were bursting at the seams. The governments were trying to reform, but perhaps it was a case of doing too little too late. Alternatively, as the famous French political philosopher, Alexis de Tocqueville, once wrote, "experience teaches that the most critical moment for bad governments is the one which witnesses their first steps toward reform."[29] It all became a matter of time ...

And yet many in the region and the West still did not believe change was forthcoming. In lectures that I gave around 2005 and 2006 based on my then unpublished manuscript of Inevitable Democracy in the Arab World, I found that the general belief was of little hope for change. Essentially, scholars and analysts were overestimating the power of the regimes and underestimating the people's frustrations and needs.

Quite bafflingly, this would continue even post-Tunisian revolution and as late as the first few days of February 2011! I recall having coffee in Beirut

---

29 Tocqueville, Alexis de, The Old Regime and the Revolution, Harper & brothers, 1856.

with an intellectual visiting from Egypt where he worked for a multinational NGO. He expressed doubts about Mubarak's departure and that if he did decide to leave the military junta would relinquish power. "I am very happy to see a revolution; but I see it very difficult to have them relinquish power once they got it."

I respectfully disagreed ...

Mubarak is alone—Literally! (February 2011)

If one thing has been shockingly revealing in the revolution unfolding in Egypt over the past two weeks, it has been the singularly faced, voiced, and embodied regime of Hosni Mubarak. Watching the coverage of the situation indelibly leaves one wondering, where on God's earth is the rest of his regime?

Aside from the very brief introduction of the newly appointed vice president rather coyly and hesitantly shaking the hand of the beleaguered autocrat, there has not been a single person representing the regime other than Mubarak himself. Not a word has been muttered by a foreign minister, minister of defense, interior, or justice. No one has seen the head of police or head of the army, a general, let alone a mayor from Cairo or Alexandria or any other Egyptian town embroiled in the uprising.

It is nothing short of incredible considering that even infamous megalomaniac dictators such as Napoleon, Hitler, Stalin, not to mention Saddam had teams around them that maintained the face of their regimes even under the most impossible of situations—sometimes even to tragically comical effects. At least in the case of Iraq, while its Foreign Minister Tarek Aziz, shuttled the world to make its case, Saddam's Information Minister Mohammad Saeed Al Sahhaf, who became known as Comical Ali, was busy claiming victory to the world!

In the case of Egypt, the rest of Mubarak's regime has been utterly silent and faceless. I can think of three possible explanations:

First, the regime echelons find themselves unable to defend the actions of the regime to which they belong. This seems to be wishful thinking; however, as in the very least it would have led to someone switching sides hoping to become a "hero" of the uprising. This hasn't happened. Indeed, considering the recent attacks on the protesters, the opposite is occurring.

Second, the regime leaders have decided to distance themselves from the octogenarian not wanting to imminently go down with him. Perhaps some even garner thoughts of succession and do not wish to see their chances eliminated through association.

The third possibility is that Mubarak quite literally is and has been a one-man show all this time, not trusting anything or anyone around him, not even ministers in his cabinet. He has basically been the head of a body-less regime surviving through foreign military aid, cronyism, and controlled violence. In his time of need, the house of cards would fall and show the autocrat to have been quite naked all along.

Regardless of which scenario is the cause for this enigma, and it may very well be a combination, keeping Mubarak around for him to save face is as much immoral as it is impractical serving no one's interest either in Egypt or outside. Mubarak may very well end up going down in history as having headed one of the most hollow regimes ever to brace the planet.

Obama needs to issue a doctrine of peaceful democratic transition (February 2011)

Throughout the Egyptian uprising, President Obama and his administration played a balancing act trying not to alienate their autocratic regional allies, while simultaneously not opposing the will of the Egyptian people. So far, this approach seems to have worked. The Egyptian regime fell, other allies in the region didn't (not yet at least), the popular revolution carried its own weight remaining relatively peaceful, and the US did not come out on the wrong side. The question now is: Will this approach continue to work as the Egyptian democracy begins the more challenging process of building itself?

The answer to this question depends on the assumption being made. If, for instance, one assumes that the source behind the revolution was simply ideological—a desire for freedom—then the fence approach may indeed be sufficient. In this case, the Obama administration would best not take center stage and instead deploy more subtle policies and behind the scenes support. This ideological assumption, however, appears incomplete at best as it fails to explain why there still seems to be discontent on the streets of Cairo and Tunis even after the autocrats have left?

A more compelling assumption perhaps is that the source of the revolution aside from the above was a tipping point reached due to several deteriorating conditions—most salient of which is the economic situation (unemployment, poverty, corruption…). If this were the case, one is bound to reach a different policy prescription since things are likely to get worse before they get any better, threatening the whole enterprise. For instance, businesses that were once associated with the regime may close their doors in the short term; and the hated economic oligarchy could flee with its money—a lot of it (both things recently occurred in Tunisia). In an effort to curtail it gross inefficiencies, the Egyptian government is likely to cut down on its spending and its employment. (In Egypt alone there are more than six million public employees, which is twice the size of the US federal government.) And so, many jobs are likely to be shed before new ones are created. Under such circumstances, poverty conditions are probably not going to improve in the short term. It is therefore no surprise that manifestations continue to occur in Egypt.

If this situation is allowed to spiral out of control, people may soon begin to question what they got themselves into. The fledgling Egyptian democracy may find itself at risk of leaving an ideological void ripe for the picking. The fear mongers' nightmare scenario lurks in the shadows.

What should the US administration do about it? For one thing, it must recognize that sitting idle or making subtle moves will not help. Once a regime has fallen, euphoria may indeed carry the nation for a few weeks, months at most. The business of building democracy and reforming, however, takes effort and money as Iraq and Afghanistan have shown. Unfortunately, between euphoria and a consolidated democracy lies a big chasm full of uncertainty and potential violence. Paying lip service during this period is a risky policy if not foolhardy—especially if we consider Egypt to be the Arab world's centerpiece.

What the US needs to do is commit to a *Peaceful Transition to Democracy Doctrine* acting as a safety net for those democratizing nations who request it. It needs to be honest and overt, showing Arab masses that the United States stands behind its democratic principles. This doctrine needs to provide substantial economic and institutional aid to help democratizing countries like Egypt, while simultaneously carrying a big stick against any sinister movements or coup attempts.

The Doctrine will serve multiple key US interests. First, it will secure these nations and keep them as strong allies. Second, it will keep the extremist elements at bay. Third, it will serve to consolidate success stories for others in the region to emulate at a fraction of what a potential war might have cost. Fourth, it would help win the hearts and minds of many Arabs and change the age-old perception that the US is hypocritically only for the autocratic regimes and against the Arab people.

Truman and Reagan's anti-communism doctrines once helped democratizing Europe face a much more menacing and dangerous foe. In their day, these doctrines were all that stood between the free world and a red one. Today, a Doctrine of Peaceful Transition to Democracy supported with generous economic aid may be what stands between true democracies in the Arab world and a chasm into a dangerous unknown. If ever there was a time for the United States to be positively engaged within the region, now is that time. Let us not shirk away from the opportunity to help under any pretext.

Libya in the balance (March 2011)

A recent article from Time Magazine highlighted the precarious situation in Libya and the fact that Gadhafi seems to be holding his ground. The question many are asking now is what to do next? The answer is one of both interests and morality.

In terms of interests, it is in US and Western interests to see Gadhafi ousted. Allowing him to remain in Libya (or a part thereof) will be a bill outstanding that will have to be paid sooner or later, not un-similar to what happened in Iraq when Saddam was kept in power in 1991. The cost and risk of keeping him will by far exceed the benefit to everyone involved and will only postpone the inevitable. If one looks at the potential risk of a single terrorist attack that he might help finance or perpetrate and the high possibility of it happening given how erratic his behavior, it would not be hard to justify his ousting. For those preaching splitting Libya with him allowed to keep the Western part, none of the above risks would be mitigated. As long as Gadhafi has at his disposal state resources—no matter what the size of the resulting state or statelet—he will pose a risk to the international community as well as his neighboring countries as he has done in the past.

This brings us to the issue of morality. Some are talking of stifling embargo with no fly zones so as to avoid outright invasion. Interestingly, few point to the fact that the deaths amounting from the embargo placed on Iraq in the 1990's exceeded by THREE FOLDS the deaths of the entire Second Iraqi War (500,000 for the first by some estimates versus 150,000 for the latter). The embargo deaths were primarily due to malnutrition of which children proved to be the victims. If the same policy is applied in Libya, would it not mean that we are punishing the entire population of Libya for the sins of a madman? And would this not be morally reprehensible? Of course, others are talking of invasion and "boots on the ground".

While it is true that invasion should not be top on the list, if indeed Gadhafi cannot be coerced to leave his country in peace, then there may be no other choice but to forcefully invade and oust him. Many are weary of this option having seen the calamities resulting from the Second Iraqi War. What other option is there since he continues his military bombardments and attacks on his people in Ajdabiya, Misrata, and elsewhere?

Having gotten involved in cases like Rwanda, Bosnia, Liberia, and East Timor ... there seems no logical reason why the US should not contemplate doing it in the case of Libya.

A speech longing to be read by an Arab leader (April 2011)

My fellow countrymen,

I stand in front of you today with two intentions. The first is simply to apologize to all of you. This may come as a surprise, for few of you would have ever expected me to do so. After much introspection, I have come to realize fully well that my rule has led you to a place few in the world would envy; and I cannot but hold myself ultimately responsible.

I apologize because while I have tried to educate you, I stifled your capacity to think.

I apologize because while I have tried to develop our nation, I failed to offer you jobs and a future your children could look forward to.

I apologize for leading your children to abandon you for distant lands.

I apologize for providing you the minimum, and then subduing your capacity to provide for yourselves.

I apologize for not controlling the corruption occurring within my regime at our nation's expense.

I apologize because under my rule, our national treasure has dried up.

I apologize for not allowing you ask for needed change.

I apologize because I have committed acts of violence against you and those you love with the false pretense of securing you.

I apologize for leading you to unjust wars that have left our nation weak and desolate and at the mercy of foreign powers.

I apologize for limiting my vision to my own survival and not that of our beloved country.

For all the above and much more, I apologize.

I stand in front of you today with a second intention. It shall be to irrevocably declare that the time has come for me to bow down and let you manage your own affairs. I do this realizing fully well the potential risks and uncertainty, but with firm confidence that if you continue to love and respect our country and fellow countrymen and women, things will turn out just fine.

My countrymen, I shall bid you farewell now and not ask for an undeserved forgiveness.

May God have mercy and always bless our country.

Islamophobia in the news (March 2011)

Lately, in the US, there seems to be a surge in what some are terming Islamophobia. A recent emotional hearing on the hill touched on the subject of Islam in America. It is being followed up by TV reports one of which is ominously called "The Muslim Next Door" running on mass media outlets like CNN.

The timing of this surge is interesting as there haven't been any recent attacks on US soil. If anything, it coincides with more alignment between fledgling democracies emerging in the Islamic Arab heartland. One would think that this should mean a reduction in Islamophobia as certain fundamental social and political principles begin to reconcile with those in the West. It hasn't happened yet. And while justification of this phobia continues to be debated, one thing is for sure, many still regard Islam as a religion to be feared because of some intrinsic incompatibility with democracy.

Some of my previous writings looked into this by delving into political, judicial, and militant Islam and what implications it has on democracy in the Arab region and the world at large. The book does so in several ways, one of which looks at non-religious institutions that have existed within Islam for more than a millennium. It does so by citing some verses that provide for religious compatibility and co-existence. It also does so by doing a comparison with the Christian world's own development and struggles. Here is a brief excerpt:

If Christianity had been so fundamental to the establishment of democracy, why was it the case that democracy as we know it today never flourished in the Christian World, until after it had escaped autocratic European persecution and found refuge in the Americas? Indeed, why is it that not until democracy flourished in the Americas and was later exported back to Europe that religious persecution—as late as the 1940's (a mere seventy years ago) and epitomized by the Jewish Holocaust—finally ceased in Europe? Was it the presence of the Christian faith that led to the establishment of sound political democracies in the West, or was it democracy that

led to the sound establishment of religious tolerance and freedom?
"Christianity" being a pre-requisite to constitutional democracy
whereas Islam is its arch nemesis is at best a historical fabrication...
A democratizing Arab world will allow a more moderate
Islam to emerge, just as it did with Christianity in
the West. In the meantime, Islam is here to stay.
The world must learn to live with it.[30]

President Obama's hands? (March 2011)

President Obama's speech yesterday night must go down in history as being one of the most "on the one hand... on the other hand" speeches in modern history. "Did the president set the proper tone and is this an introduction into what can be termed as the Obama Doctrine?" pundits are asking.

Well, on the one hand (!), there should be no question the US President is having to work within the confines of some difficult constraints—not least of which are the teetering US economy, the two wars in Afghanistan and in Iraq, a war weary American nation, and of course continuing to support friendly regional autocrats.

On the other hand, by their very definition, dictators rule with nothing but a FIRM hand, and any "other hand" presented to them is a gift of an opportunity to fight another day. Theirs is an existential fight and there is no other hand to consider. This gives them an implicit advantage over uncertainty. Their goal is one and one alone: survival, no matter how ugly it gets. Saddam preferred to remain in power notwithstanding the 500,000 Iraqi children deaths that resulted from the embargo slapped on his nation during the 1990's. The only hands he cared for were those assuring his and his regime's survival.

Long before him history had been littered with dictators and victims of their intransigence. Churchill warned of Hitler's sinister intentions at a time when the international community preferred to present the Führer

---

30 Yafi, Wissam, Inevitable Democracy in the Arab World, Palgrave Macmillan, 2012, pg. 148.

with "other hands". It resulted in the deaths of millions and incalculable destruction. The wily Brit proved to be equally prescient when he warned during the Potsdam conference of the impending Stalinist Iron Wall. Again a historic miscalculation resulted in a Cold War that lasted for half a century. Of course, Truman eventually realized the gravity of leaving the Soviets to their own devices and introduced the Truman Doctrine essentially eliminated any "other hand" and stood in support of every freedom seeking nation. Arguably it was this doctrine and the clarity of its vision, goals, and indeed the resources placed at its disposal that would lead half a century later to Soviet disintegration.

This brings us back to the Obama speech. Knowing Libya's Gadhafi and what he and his brutal regime are capable of, any "other hand" dealt to him will likely result in more pain and suffering by his people and eventually higher costs to remove him. Recent events tend to prove this as experts state that had the international community moved three weeks earlier when the rebels were on the outskirts of Tripoli, Gadhafi would have been gone by now. Instead he was given the opportunity to regroup and push back the rebels almost wiping them out. Of course, when the no-fly zone finally came, it came at a cost in the hundreds of millions of dollars and in itself was no guarantee to seeing him leave. This is leading some to question whether giving Gadhafi an ultimatum would not finally lead him to see the futility of his fight. It might very well. Unfortunately, an ultimatum such as this is not likely to come if the threat to his existence comes from the rebels whom he feels he can destroy. Rather, it has to come from the international community whom he fears. And it is here that Obama's speech and indeed his Doctrine, may fall short of the support needed prolonging the inevitable but causing more unnecessary pain, loss and destruction in the interim.

What was missing from Obama's speech was perhaps a clearer *Peaceful Transition to Democracy Doctrine* that promises to support any nation in the Middle East and North Africa who decide to overthrow their dictators. Nothing short of this will size up to the challenges and indeed opportunities an inevitably democratizing Arab world present to America and the world. It is time for President Obama to limit options to one hand—and that is shackles for the dictators' hands.

What happens now? (April 2011)

In some of my recent lectures, I have been repeatedly receiving the same questions: "With Yemen's Saleh, Libya's Gadhafi, and Syria's Assad desperately and brutally clinging on to power, what happens now? Is the region headed towards a reversal of its uprising? Will all of it come to naught nipped in the bud by these obstinate regimes and the interests behind them?"

The answer is quite simply: no. It is taking time as it perhaps must, the general trend is irreversible. The issue was never security or the monopoly of violence these regimes wield over their populations. The primary argument in the book is that the dynamics that brought about all these uprisings include geopolitical, geoeconomic, geosocial and technological variables—most of which the regimes have little if any control over. Post uprising, these variables are all still firmly in place and in fact have become even more acute playing differing degrees of influence within the revolting nations. In Yemen, for example, poverty remains rampant, unemployment high, neither of which with any potential for alleviation from an incessantly growing population. If anything the recent unrest is bound to aggravate the situation, economically speaking. Not even the Gulf's counterweight (a potential geopolitically opposing force in this case) has been able to reverse events in Yemen. Actually, the GCC countries finally decided last week to come out calling for Yemen's Saleh to step down—a clear indication that they concluded if events cannot be reversed they might as well end up on the winning side.

In Syria, the Assad regime's internal struggle manifests itself almost daily with schizophrenic policies calling one day for the release of all jailed protesters and shooting at them the next. But again as in Yemen, Assad's Syria has dynamics at play that are also irreversible. The fact that it all started in Daraa—one of the poorest regions in Syria—is no coincidence. Poverty and youth unemployment and mass dissatisfaction with the regime's governance over the past 4 decades have all culminated in a force that has overcome the military and technological impediments that the regime put in place attempting to stop protesters from converging. If anything, the draconian measures that Assad's regime has put in place are bound to make the economic situation worse eventually and inevitably leading to a total collapse. Again in this case, neither Iranian support nor ironically Israeli covert support (some have suggested The Devil You Know Theory that Israel is worried that an Assad replacement regime could pose an even greater threat to its status quo in the Golan) are likely to reverse the desperate needs or wants of the wretched portions within Syria.

And finally we come to Gadhafi's Libya. There, the geopolitical shifts in Egypt to the East, Tunisia to the West, and NATO from above have all but sealed the eccentric dictator's fate. Add to that his brutal killing and bombing of civilians in opposition cities, and the slightest chance of reconciliation has disappeared. It is not surprising that Europe, which one would expect would have preferred generally a geopolitical status quo in Libya, has been leading the charge in calling for his ouster and very recently complete regime change—completely reversing its opposition to this policy. And still Gadhafi hangs on. The only shame is that he insists on spilling his countrymen and women's blood in his grand exit, almost forcing the end game to be his and his family's own demise not dissimilar to that of Saddam. It would come as no surprise if eventually NATO ends this whole rouse with a bombing to get rid of him once and for all.

It is natural for the incumbent regimes to attempt to hang on to power, which for years has brought them and their cliques power and riches. The game is up unfortunately; and anything they attempt to do to prolong their hold over power will ironically aggravate an already tenuous situation in their societies as it has done in Tunisia and Egypt. The dynamics in place are simply irreversible. The sooner the dictators realize this and relinquish power, the better the eventual outcome for their societies. This may seem wishful thinking, and it may very well be. But in truth, there really is nothing else they can do, certainly not killing and maiming.

Wanted: Entrepreneurship in the Arab world (April 2011)

Within the context of regional needs going forward, I was recently asked in a lecture why the Lebanese are so entrepreneurial.

The answer is quite simple. They have had to be. Throughout their history they have either been on the fringe of governance or without it.

155

My grandfather, Ghaleb, who is said to have studied in Boston in the early 20th century returned to a pre-independence Ottoman ruled Lebanon. He was politically prosecuted and had to flee for safety and to be able to make a living. He immigrated to Bombay in Raj India where he established a lucrative textile trade.

My father in his turn studied in England and upon his return started an education business, only to be thwarted by Lebanon's civil war. His creativity could not be stifled, and he moved to a barren Dubai in the early 70's where he continued with his business.

Similarly, I had to leave Lebanon to the US at an early age to finish my education. I started my own high tech business right after school. My son already displays some entrepreneurship traits by teaching his old man new social media trends and faux pas...

Our story is by no means exceptional. We are but another Lebanese family, which for one reason or another has had to turn to its own devices because the setting from which it came did not provide one. We are a product of our environment and I tend to think if it is not yet in our genes, in the very least, it is well engrained in our psyche. We have become what we inevitably have had to.

What has all this got to do with the Middle East's new realities? It is all about self-reliance. Developed nations are as wealthy as they are because they have managed to maximize the productivity of the micro-elements within their societies making them self-reliant not to mention prosperous. Some falsely claim that large businesses control the United States. While they do exert considerable influence, 80% of employment actually comes from small businesses. According to the US Small Business Administration, there are more than 24 million small businesses in the United States as compared to about 50,000 large ones. The story is very similar in places such as Germany and Japan. Developing places such as Brazil, South Africa, and China point to a similar trend. Self-reliance appears to be a necessary and perhaps sufficient step to prosperity.

This brings us back to the new realities in the Middle East. Unless nations in the Arab World begin to seriously develop their micro-elements, these societies will increasingly face difficulties as they democratize and liberalize.

SECTION FOUR: ARAB SPRING

Self-sufficiency has to replace government welfare. The sooner this is realized the less painful the inevitable shift will be. Entrepreneurship may not be the panacea, but it sure as heck is a good option when government handouts dry up as they are bound to.

The eventual fate of Arab dictators and its significance (April 2011)

Two recent developments give conflicting messages as to the impending fate of dethroned dictators in the Arab World and its regional democratization implications.

On the one hand, Egypt has had Mubarak and his family under house arrest since his ouster. They are being investigated for both widespread corruption charges as well as ordering the killing of protestors. One Egyptian minister recently went as far as stating that if "ordering the killings charge is proven, it would imply the death penalty". This points to two significant developments: First, that the matter is being taken seriously by Egyptian institutions which appear to be following what one would hope is legal due process. Second and more importantly, that the Egyptian uprising is behind this, because in reality no one in the military junta or the international community would particularly benefit from persecuting Mubarak. It is being prodded by the people themselves who are asking for justice and accountability. This bodes well on Egypt and its revolution, which continues to surprise many in its perseverance and wisdom.

On the other hand we have Yemen, where Saleh's departure is being "negotiated" by Saudi Arabia and other GCC members. Essentially, the agreement is a barter exchange: Relinquishing power for immunity from persecution. This agreement, however, does not appear to be supported by the Yemeni people as the sit-ins remain firmly in place after its announcement—with a tendency to increase. The latest news from Yemen is that new crackdowns are meant to force the people to disperse and accept this agreement. This carries potential negative implications for the future institutionalization of democracy in that country. Essentially it attempts to force an expedient state of amnesia on a nation that has suffered at the hands of its dictator for the better part of 30 years. If it is enforced, with time it is bound to come back and bite one way or another. The Yemeni's are demanding what they want—justice and accountability—but are patronizingly being given pocket change by the GCC. Only giving in to their demands in their entirety will be sufficient to quell their massive demonstrations setting them on their way to a functional democracy. Trying to snuff the uprising will backfire sooner or later.

Early steps at institutionalizing democracy, part of which is holding the dictators accountable, can have massive effects and path dependence trajectories. Now is not the time for expediency nor is it the time to circumvent proper procedures to bring the corrupt and the brutal dictators in the Arab World to justice. The uprisings are demanding it because in their mass wisdom, they realize it has got to be the beginning of a long and arduous healing and democratizing process for their battered societies. This Egypt admirably seems to be doing quite well.

Splintering terrorism (May 2011)

In September of 1993, I happened to be in Medellin, Colombia of all places. I recall quite well it was a very wet and rainy day in what was known at the time as the drug capital of the world. That morning one of the most wanted criminals in the world, Pablo Escobar, made a phone call to his son. It would cost him his life. At the time, he had been living in hiding for several years and some reports had said he had been sighted as far as Brazil. Others reported that he had completely changed his face. Turns out none of it was true. The phone call was intercepted by the CIA and Colombian intelligence and traced to a regular townhouse in a regular residential area in the middle of Medellin. He had been hiding out in the open all along. An elite Colombian force was dispatched, a firefight ensued, and the infamous Escobar was no more.

This story was almost replicated a couple of days ago. This time the global manhunt was on Bin Laden. Again, a phone call was intercepted by the CIA, but this time an American elite force was dispatched to get the work done and Bin Laden became a part of world's history books.

Some are beginning to question what will happen to Al Qaeda now that Bin Laden is gone. Perhaps looking at what happened to Medellin's infamous drug cartel can shed some light.

Upon Escobar's death, there was a power struggle with other regional cartels (Cali and the Colombian Coast cartels). This led to some infighting that eliminated Escobar's henchmen and closest partners. What eventually ensued were dozens and sometimes even hundreds of mini capos that currently for all intents and purposes do not appear on any major radar. The monopoly of the trade splintered into many pieces. This did not necessarily reduce from the amount of the drug trade per se. What it did reduce, however, is any national sovereignty threat. None of these new drug splinter groups were big enough as Escobar had been to threaten the whole nation. Their mantra of survival became keeping their heads down.

The world of global terrorism is likely to witness something very similar. On the one hand, post Bin Laden Al Qaeda still has henchmen such as Al Zawahiri and others. But none at this point appear to be capable of taking over the mantle nor may have the funding for it—that is unless one of Bin Laden's surviving sons decides to try his luck. As unlikely as this may seem, in that part of the world one never knows... Most likely, however, the organization not unlike the Colombian cartels in the 1990's will splinter into many smaller groups. As a matter of fact this had started occurring even before Bin Laden's death. The reason for this quite simply is geographic coverage. Unable to communicate effectively over such a huge Islamic expanse, the only way for the organization to work was for it to decentralize, and it did so. This splintering process is likely to accelerate now that Bin Laden is gone. This may mean two things: First, that Al Qaeda is not likely to disappear. Second, and more ominously, terrorism is likely to continue.

Interestingly, in the case of drug imports, the United States seems to be resigned to an acceptable range of imports. Completely eradicating drugs has proven to be exorbitant and impractical. The question to ask now is whether or not there would be an "acceptable" equivalent in terms of terrorism?

This is a question only the future can answer, but a democratizing Arab world, which consolidates Arab states and has them responding to the needs of their citizens will certainly prove to be an antidote against a splintered Al Qaeda.

Bin Laden's legacy: Che or Hitler (May 2011)

A recent US article wondered why the Islamic World has been so quiet concerning the killing of Bin Laden.

In the West, the case seems rather clear cut. While more knowledgeable analysts will admit that we in the United States in a way helped create the Bin Laden phenomenon by training and supporting his initial activities in Afghanistan during the Soviet era, most no doubt see him purely in light of the 9/11 calamity—an abominable figure that will go down in history as having committed a heinous crime. Hence his death caused celebrations and dancing in the streets of Washington, D.C., rarely seen by other occurrences much more significant in geopolitical terms—such as the fall of the Soviet Empire for instance.

While no one in the Islamic and Arab region is likely to deny the gravity of Bin Laden's 9/11 crimes (although some conspiracy thinkers still manage to doubt its authenticity), they see it from a lens not as acute as the crime itself—as horrendously tragic as it were. Having lived their own history, their lens is a bit wider, encompassing other elements in the overall picture. What are some of these elements? First and foremost, the autocratic regimes in the region and the injustices they have committed towards their people for decades. Second, Western Realpolitik, which is seen as having turned a blind eye, ruthlessly was using the region for its own geopolitical and geoeconomic interests. Others see Bin Laden's Islamic militant brand itself as a revolutionary response to incompetence and corruption not unlike some religious reformational movements that happened during other periods in history—albeit few would wish or even contemplate having a Taliban-style governing system. And finally, some see Bin Laden, for better or worse, as having been a catalyst who forced the region to daringly demand what it had never dared to and face-up to who it had never faced up to. They ask, if regional regimes and their Western backers have justified their means for their Near East regional ends killing millions of innocent in the process, wasn't Bin Laden essentially guilty of the same?

And so the quiet acquiescence of the Arab region in a way may be introspective. While feeling ashamed at all the pain and suffering that Bin laden had caused, there may be a lingering sympathy related to what he was trying to attain—a breakup of the vicious cycle that had incumbent autocratic regimes and the West colluding at the expense of the region's people themselves. That the break did eventually occur with the US's bold invasion and forceful democratization of Iraq and more recently the Arab world's uprisings may vindicate this argument—albeit in itself eventually making Bin Laden a rather irrelevant figure. One Emirati Professor may have summed it up nicely by stating "Bin Laden died in Egypt before being killed in Pakistan."

From a regional perspective, Bin Laden as a historical figure may very well end up going down in history as having been more a Che Guevara-type of figure than a Serbia's Milosevic, Rwanda's Kabuka, let alone a Stalin or a Hitler. They may not be willing to admit this just about yet. Hence the quiet.

Lessons from Soviet Hungary hardline Arab regimes (May 2011)

Democratizing a nation while facing hardline regimes has never been easy. As the Syrian, Yemeni, and Libyan regimes seem entrenched and not willing to let go of power to the people, perhaps they can benefit from recent experiences from Eastern Europe, of which Hungary stands out as a good example.

As the Soviet Empire began disintegrating in the late 1980's, stifled Hungarians, who had been ruled by the Communists for far too many decades had grown tired of the single-party system. While democratic opposition groups were splintered, by 1989 most agreed that the priority was seeing their political system opened. They began pressuring the communist regime and succeeded in coalescing thousands of demonstrators in the streets to pressure the incumbent communist regime. The communist government tried to control and channel the emerging dialogue, but failed as the democratic parties refused to acquiesce to a multitude of political offers, bribes, and divide and rule tactics. Ideologically disparate, the opposition parties decided to maintain a united democratic front.

Over the next several months, the communist regime itself began feeling the pressure from within with some party members taking a more reformist position. Somewhat counter-intuitively, the split ended up occurring within the ruling party. A posterior shuffle within the communist party eventually led to a more reformist party leadership, and this in turn paved the way for a roundtable discussion with the opposition.

In her insightful book, The Walls Came Tumbling Down, Gale Stokes writes:

> "By mid-1989, free elections were no longer an issue in Hungary, but almost everything else was. During the roundtable discussions the [ruling] party concentrated on economic problems, hoping to get the opposition to share responsibility for a deteriorating economic situation and for unpopular reforms that would be needed to correct it. The opposition insisted on presenting political demands, such as eliminating Workers Guards, which were an armed force in every factory, and getting party cells out of the workplace. After three months of difficult negotiations, in September 1989 the conferees agreed to overhaul the legal system, depoliticize the army, and cut the size and competence of the Workers Guards."

One contentious issue did remain and it was whether Hungary would have a strong president voted for by the people—which the Communists wanted—or whether it would have a weaker one voted for by the parliament. This issue could not be solved by the roundtable discussion, but rather saw a referendum called for, which out of four million votes, saw the latter group come on top by a mere 6,100 votes! The parliamentary elections that followed early in 1990, saw the people massively vote against the Communists giving them only 8.5% of the parliamentary seats. The new parliament proceeded to vote for a non-communist president.

Hungary's case provides several lessons to the impending transformation occurring throughout the Middle East. First, the ruling regime as expected tries to maintain its powers by attempting to institutionalize the single party rule [communism for instance] and other trickery, such as the "Workers Guards", who typically are not there to protect the workers as much as to spy on them. The opposition groups did not fall for it and insisted on political reform before any economic reform under the single party system. This was smart for a couple of reasons: It kept the pressure on the regime; and if the economic situation got any better, the incumbent totalitarian regime would feel even less likely to leave power.

Secondly, as a reaction to firm political opposition, the ruling regime itself began to see different strands emerge within its own rank and file. Hardliners were left with an impossible dilemma: If they imposed their power, it aggravated the situation on the streets as is happening in Syria and Libya. If, however, they allowed reformers to emerge within the party, then they knew there was no hope either. Their days became numbered one way or the other.

Thirdly, once the ruling regime realized that change was imminent, it preferred to negotiate with the democratic proponents than to stamp out the protests. This saved Hungary from an even larger calamity. In Libya, it appears Gadhafi has issued an "over my dead body" edict. His end may be near as a result of it. In Syria, Assad still has the chance to remedy the situation if he introduces some reformers, but even then, in all likelihood his regime's days are numbered.

And finally, if negotiations with democratizers are launched as they have been in Egypt, while they may be difficult and will take time, they will inevitably lead to the peaceful emergence of liberalization and democratization as they did in Hungary against a regime much more powerful than any of the Arab ones.

The people are on the right side of history. Patience and perseverance will pay off... inevitably.

An imperfect democracy is what makes it a perfect one (May 2011)

Having studied profoundly the American democracy, I find its genius was not in its original design (notwithstanding its brilliance), but rather in its ability to continuously reinvent and realign itself with its north star—the interests of its citizens.

A democracy, very much like a plane, is statically imperfect and weighs heavy. Its perfection comes only when it is in motion, with all its elements in harmonious balance, and transporting it to a destination, which by design it is never meant to reach. Rather the goal is to keep flying.

On this the 235th anniversary of the United States revolution, which reintroduced democracy to the world after a very long absence, it is befitting to study and quote some of the salient founding fathers:

*"Democratical states must always feel before they can see:
it is this that makes their governments slow, but the people
will be right at last... When a people shall have become
incapable of governing themselves, and fit for a master, it
is of little consequence from what quarter he comes."*
GEORGE WASHINGTON, Letter to Marquis de Lafayette,
July 25, 1785 and April 28, 1788 respectively

*"It has ever been my hobby-horse to see rising in America an
empire of liberty, and a prospect of two or three hundred millions of
freemen, without one noble or one king among them. You say it is
impossible. If I should agree with you in this, I would still say, let us
try the experiment, and preserve our equality as long as we can."*
JOHN ADAMS, To Count Starsfield, February 3, 1786

*"I have no fear that the result of our experiment will be that
men may be trusted to govern themselves without a master.
Could the contrary of this be proved, I should conclude either
that there is no God or that He is a malevolent being."*
THOMAS JEFFERSON, Letter to David Hartley, 1787

"We may define a [democratic] republic ... as a government which derives all its powers directly or indirectly from the great body of the people, and is administered by persons holding their offices during pleasure, for a limited period, or during good behavior. It is essential to such government that it be derived from the great body of the society, not from an inconsiderable proportion, or a favored class of it."

JAMES MADISON, The Federalist Papers, 1788

Can the Syrian regime overcome its uprising? (June 2011)

There are many who believe the Assad's Syrian regime has what it takes to overcome the current crisis. "It has many hidden cards still to play!" they claim. The Syrian regime itself on regional TV stations seems confident it can. The problem with this thinking is that it disregards four key realities (elements)[31]:

First the geopolitical situation. The regime's action over the past two months seems to indicate that it is indeed stuck in a different era. During the 1970's, Syria was surrounded with autocrats, supported by a mighty Soviet Union, and very much facing an expansionist Israel. The regime thrived. But none of these factors exist anymore. Syria is now surrounded by emerging albeit fledgling democracies, its major benefactor, the Soviet Union, disintegrated two decades ago, and Israel's expansionist policies excepting settlements have all but ceased. All Syria can count on now is Iran's support. Unfortunately, this may prove more a liability than an asset, both internally and internationally. Besides, Iran itself has enough to cope with facing a serious embargo and dealing with its own internal turmoil.

Secondly and thirdly, the geosocial and geoeconomic situation have also substantially deteriorated. Syria has ballooned to a population of almost 25 million most of whom are youth. Unfortunately, the country's archaic economic structure based on an expired centralized planning model has

---

31 A more detailed analysis can be found in Inevitable Democracy in the Arab World, Palgrave MacMillan, 2012.

failed. The few reforms that have been promised and the fewer still that have been implemented are nowhere near what is needed for the country to get back on its feet. With the little oil it had having almost dried up, the current regime has no immediate remedies let alone ideas of how to resolve the current economic calamity. The longer the uprising carries on affecting directly needed tourism and trade, the worse things are likely to get.

Fourthly, even though the regime has tried its best to muffle any news coming out of the country, technology has managed to keep a link between the people and the outside world disseminating news of the regime's violence. Social media connectivity, mobile connectivity, and satellite have all kept the protestors in touch between themselves and with the outside world. Short of calamitously shutting down all telephone and internet communications, the regime can really do nothing about this.

And so the question I usually ask to those who theorize that the regime has "many hidden cards left to play" is: What exactly are these cards? The regime has shown its hand to its people and the world at large and no one likes it. Ironically even Putin, a product of the Soviet era and a leader not known to mince words, pointing to Syria recently stated, "In the modern world it is impossible to use political instruments of 40 years ago."

These are indeed changing times where all cards are out in the open, and bluffing quite futile. The sooner the Syrian regime and its mouth pieces realize this, the better it is for all. Change is inevitable.

Princes or paupers in the Arab spring (June 2011)

In recent news and analysis (the most recent of which was published in *The New York Times*), Saudi Arabia has reportedly been trying to fend off the region's revolutions with its own counter-revolution. "We're sending a message that monarchies are not where this is happening," Prince Waleed bin Talal al-Saud of the Saudi royal family was quoted as saying rather assuredly. "We are not trying to get our way by force, but to safeguard our interests." This has been followed up by reports that Saudi Arabia has been spending billions in Egypt, Yemen, and Bahrain trying to keep a semblance of what once was.

It is rather bemusing to think that Saudi Arabia actually thinks it can do anything about the concurrent revolutions. Even the mighty United States came to that quick realization during the last days of Mubarak's reign abandoning their long-time ally in favor of what was inevitably going to be a popular victory. And yet some in Saudi Arabia rather Don Quixotesquely believe they can fight the windmill of change. Perhaps their optimism comes from believing that all that has to be done is simply repeat the policies of the 1960's when the kingdom vehemently opposed Nasser's and other populist movements in the region.

This rather simplistic associational argument is oblivious of the regional sea change that has occurred over the past 40 years from a geopolitical, geoeconomic, geosocial, and technological standpoint. The world today is quite different. There is no longer a communist threat, meaning the Arab people themselves in their revolutions are not against the interests of the West as some Arab communist revolutionaries may have been back in the 1960's. On the contrary, the youth leading charge see themselves very much as part of a globalized world. They seek the same freedoms the United States and other Western nations enjoy. Saudi Arabia has nothing to offer them in such soft power terms. Geoeconomically and geosocially, the region itself is in a shambles and in need of massive reform. The Arab population continues to burgeon and is in dire need of opportunities and jobs—something which Saudi Arabia has not even figured out for its own population. Official Saudi reports place their own unemployment rate at 10%, which is considered a gross underestimate of the actual, especially among the youth. But even if we took the Saudi figure at face value, it means there are hundreds of thousands of jobless youth with no future and no voice to ask for any. Saudi Arabia's own economic woes are not an example with which it can lead the region.

Neither are its social ills. Half of its population (women) is not allowed to work fully yet (granted there has been recent improvement), and the other half due to numbing government subsidies has not had to be as productive as it needed to be. In fact, every trip to Saudi Arabia one indelibly reads reports of Saudi policy focus on Saudization, which is the term used to replace foreign expat labor with Saudi locals signifying the challenges that the kingdom is facing. This is hardly an economic system that can be exported to a region so direly in need of micro-productivity, entrepreneurial activity, and employment opportunities. And finally on the technological side, any form of censorship has been muffled due to advances in Satellite communication, mobile telephony, and the Internet. In my book, *Inevitable Democracy in the Arab World*, I mention some anecdotes from within Saudi on the very subject highlighting the futility of any form of censorship in this day and age.

A report recently listed Prince Waleed bin Talal as the most powerful Arab on the globe. Perhaps this power tends to give a person a sense of confidence to tackle any problem. Unfortunately, the Arab region's calamity is one problem neither Waleed nor the kingdom as a whole can resolve, nor can any nation for that matter. In fact, at the time, I argued that each Arab nation will have to resolve its problem one citizen at a time giving them self-determination but also exerting on them self-sufficiency. For that to happen indigenous reform is needed not stifling. Saudi Arabia would stand to benefit if it realized that it cannot begin reforming its own society by impeding everyone else from reforming their own.

Ironically, in the very same report, which listed Bin Talal as the most powerful Arab, Wael Ghonim, the Egyptian mid-manager credited with enabling the Egyptian uprising, was listed as the second most influential. This has led some to state that power and money still rule. Actually, their conclusion is wrong. For in the region, there are only a few handfuls of billionaires such as Waleed, but there are potentially 300 million Waels out there.

If I were in Waleed's shoes, I would not bet against the Arab revolutions nor spend my money impeding them. Instead, I would try to find ways to invest in reform, especially inside of Saudi Arabia—reform which would improve the livelihood of the good Saudi people.

On the impossibility of reforming incumbent Arab regimes (July 2011)

In the research I have conducted throughout these years, it has become clear to me that incumbent Arab regimes cannot reform—even if they needed to—because it is essentially a self-inflicting exercise. There are multiple justifications for this:

First, they stand to lose the most from change because it was essentially a zero sum game (what society needs, they have to give up in concessions).

Second, assuming the regime still manages to find the goodwill to reform, skyrocketing entropic rates within the regimes due to increasing corruption, nepotism, and massive government payrolls makes it all but impossible to carry through any serious reform without alienating others within the ruling regime—especially the hardliners. The best one could hope for from them is a semblance of reform with carefully paced change. Indeed, by making change eternally slow, their hope was to ultimately avoid it. It didn't work; and I argued as far back as 2005 through published Op-Eds that it wasn't change that needed to be paced, but rather pace that needed to be changed.

Third, is the age of most of these regimes, most of which have been around for decades. These are not the vibrant catalysts needed, nor will they be willing to take risks that could come back and undermine their own power.

Fourth, they simply do not have the knowhow (let alone inclination); and those who do have generally been either jailed, executed, or otherwise banished.

I found it quite laughable at the apex of the uprising in Egypt to see some suggesting that a regime such as Mubarak's should be expected to carry out any meaningful reform. Not only was the man an octogenarian, he had been in power for three decades and not done it. The regime did try on some fronts in the middle of the last decade, especially on the economic front. But it made sure it kept things in check, especially on the political front. When it finally realized the magnitude of the problem following the January 2011 uprising, it was too late.

There is really no reason to believe that fundamentally hollow Arab regimes such as Syria, Libya, and Yemen could possibly hope to fare any better.

Somalia: Yet another tragic Arab story (July 2011)

As Libya, Syria, Yemen and Egypt battle for democratic survival, Somalia is facing a battle even more grave—that of famine. Approximately 1.5 million Somalis are currently teetering on the brink. Interestingly enough, and rather counter-intuitively, according to recent reports, this famine is not due solely to climactic conditions or to a shortage of food. Rather, it is due to a failed state that has been unable to provide for its citizens—even when it has received aid that is earmarked for that purpose. The world is now scampering trying to figure out solutions to alleviate the Somali people's hunger.

If nothing else Somalia is a sad case study for the entire region of what falling into anarchy and disorder would look like and what it could result in.

Gadhafi: A shame for the whole world to bear (August 2011)

A mere few months ago Gadhafi and his family could boast of billions (with a capital B) and outright ownership of Libya. He is now a worthless fugitive running for his life, two of his sons having reportedly lost theirs, and many members of his family having fled a burning nation. The question that begs itself is whether or not it had to be this way?

Gadhafi could have negotiated a settlement and walked away with billions, but didn't. Instead he chose to stay put and fight against the most powerful of global military coalitions—NATO—with fledgling mercenaries from poor neighboring African countries. The reasons for this seemingly irrational behavior are not for certain. One could contemplate a complete detachment from the factual—with those around him preferring not to state the obvious to him. His ludicrous and vociferous sons claiming inevitable victory tend to support this theory. Perhaps over the years, the regime's upper echelons had begun believing their own web of lies and hyperboles.

Then again his choice may shed light on the theory that he is indeed a madman—a Neroesque sort of character who preferred to watch Libya burn and laugh at the spectacle even if he himself inevitably forgoes all the riches and gets killed in the process. After all, faced with the choice of walking away with billions or almost certain death for himself and members of his family, who in their right state of mind would choose the later? Better yet, who would choose it after seeing what had happened to Saddam and his sons, Mubarak and his sons, Ben Ali and his family ... And yet as irrational as it may seem, to men like Gadhafi, the rationality of preferring to live in obscurity to them would be the irrational choice—that is over dying in the limelight, even if it means taking their whole family down with them.

Regardless of the reasons, Gadhafi made a choice, and his family and he will pay for it. The world should not feel sorry for the whole lot. What the civilized world should feel sorry for are the lives of all those innocent civilians that have been lost as a result of his actions, and for having allowed such a man to rule his nation unopposed for so long. As mass graves resulting from his regime begin to be unearthed, it will be a shame not only for Libya to bear, but the world at large—especially those nations, which were affected by his violence and yet continued to deal with him. That perhaps was the greatest shame of all.

A dictator's inevitable fate (October 2011)

Another Arab dictator bites the dust... Of course some say Gadhafi had a choice between "walking away" with billions and "dying"... Did he really? I tend to think not. He chose the latter not because he was an irrational idiot (although he appeared to be one at times), nor because of a supreme belief in a cause (there was none); and certainly not because of any suicidal wish (for himself and members of his family).

Rather, it seems to have been a rational decision because deep down he knew that the day he would step out of power—no matter how much money he had—would be the day his regime's atrocities would catch up with him. His rational choice simply tried to postpone the inevitable to the last minute ... his dying words reportedly were "Don't shoot!"

They did shoot to kill as he had done to thousands before him.

His inevitable fate had finally caught up with him.

Islam need not be feared (June 2012)

In his monumental book Democracy in America written in the early part of the 19th century and describing the details of America's democracy (at a time when Europe had none), Alexis de Tocqueville wrote:

> *"How is it possible that society should escape destruction if the moral tie is not strengthened in proportion as the political tie is relaxed? And what can be done with a people who are their own masters if they are not submissive to the Deity?"*[32]

In a recent lecture I gave, a person in the audience expressed trepidation of the role that Islamists were now playing in a democratizing Arab region. "It appears that they are taking over," the Lebanese man stated forebodingly. Interestingly, this same anxiety was voiced again in a book-reading I held shortly after across the globe. A lady from Tunisia and one from Egypt expressed the same concerns having seen the results of the elections and the rise of Islamist presidents to lead their respective nations. I found it interesting but not surprising to hear them express these concerns. After all, any change is bound to tag along a certain amount of uncertainty. After years under unrelentingly stale and very restrictive regimes, I rationalized that if anything Arab societies should be feeling a lot more from the anxiety sudden change brings than societies where change had become a constant. And yet while I may sympathize with this anxiety, I do not share in the fear—not for the time being at least. There are several reasons for this.

Before getting into this, perhaps it is important to clarify some nomenclature. First, Islam is different from Islamists, which in turn is different from Islamic extremism. As I tend to prefer simple things, I regard Islam as the religion and its set of beliefs; Islamists as groups who base their actions and policies on the tenets of Islam; and Islamic extremists as offshoots resulting from either persisting unresolved grievance or warped of ideology.

---

32 De Tocqueville, Alexis, Democracy in America, Volume I, 1835.

If we take Islam per se, one does not tend to find regional fear from the religion itself in the Arab World. Indeed, it has been argued rather successfully that no proof exists pointing to Islam as being a more violent religion—be it qualitatively or quantitatively. The fact that minorities have been living within Islam for more than a millennium and Islam has been coexisting side by side with the world's faiths should be proof enough of conviviality not only in theory but in practice. It is hard to fathom that this would suddenly change. Indeed, the fact that Islam does not have a single religious authority—as say Catholicism with the Pope—makes it all but impossible.

When it comes to Islamists and their politics—as opposed to Islam as a religion—again it would be hard for anyone to argue ex ante that they are necessarily going to transform their societies into theocracies potentially causing havoc to their communities. Indeed theocracy per se in the Arab world, and contrary to popular belief, has almost never existed, not even under the Caliphate, which is considered by most serious Islamic scholars as more of a constitutional republic than a theocracy. Today, in the entire Arab world, there is not a single theocracy. Actually in the entire Islamic world (including all the non-Arab states), there is basically only one, Iran. Therefore there is no reason to believe that all of a sudden, emerging Arab democracies or Islamist parties will follow-suit and theocratize their nations. Indeed, for such an unusual occurrence to happen one would expect to see the influence of some supreme religious leaders who could be blindly followed—similar to Ayatollah Khomeini in Iran for instance—but in the Arab world there isn't. In fact, there cannot be such a figure, because religious authority in Islam, by the religion's own design, was purposely dissipated to pretty much avoid this from happening.

This brings us to Islamic extremism, which has been a modern phenomenon. Here, we also need to differentiate between extremist strands borne out of unresolved grievance (such as Hamas in Palestine, Hezbollah in Lebanon, and the FIS in Algeria) and warped ideological strands (such as the Afghani Taliban and Al Qaeda). The first group of extremists has proven to be national in scope. While they have fought wars, none have exceeded nor have destroyed the democracies in which they exist. Hamas continues to exist and deal with the PLO—and even with Israel—in the Palestinian Territories, Hezbollah has been politically active in Lebanon for the past two decades, and the FIS ended its war with the Algerian government once its grievances were met. This brings us to the warped ideologues such as the Taliban, which changed the face of Afghanistan, and Al Qaeda, which caused immeasurable damage to the world and indeed the Islamic and Arab worlds. Again there is no proof that any Arab nation is about to adopt such ideology, and if it did, it is hard to believe that the nation will not descend into civil strife with the people supported by the world community. Saudi Arabia, Egypt, Jordan, Iraq, and Lebanon have all battled Islamic extremists. While the war may not be over against extremism, the extremists have dwindled and it would be hard to imagine how their societies would all of a sudden decide to accept being ruled under such an ideology—be they Salafists or otherwise.

So if Islamic extremism as a system is highly unlikely, it leaves us with potential Islamist parties politically in the democratic fray with everyone else. Sounds pretty much like the United States' democracy with its religious right, Europe with its Christian Democrats, Turkey with its conservative Islamists, and Israel with its Orthodox Jews, doesn't it?

Going back to Tocqueville's democratic analysis of the West he concluded, *"Despotism may govern without faith, but liberty cannot."*[33] Why should anyone conclude anything differently for the Arab World? Islam need not be feared; for its role in the Arab World is as inevitable.

Pan-Arabism is dead, Long live Pan-Arabism (July 2012)

With Syria in the throes of a vicious civil war, some have begun ringing the death knell of Pan-Arabism. Not coincidentally, those siding with the embattled Syrian regime have expressed fear that if the current war leads to the ousting of the Assad regime, it will mean that the last bastion of "Al Orouba", or Pan-Arabism, will have fallen. Those who counter suggest that Pan-Arabism has been suffering from a long and slow death; and the only

---

33 De Tocqueville, Alexis, Democracy in America, Volume I, 1835.

reason for its unremitting usage by autocrats is to Machiavelically divert the people's attention from their regime's dismal failures.

Regardless of their merits, both arguments may be missing a key point: Is Pan-Arabism a static concept? In other words, is Pan-Arabism of last century the same as one that may exist today—or more importantly in the future? I think not. Traditional Pan-Arabism—with its colonial rejectionism and militarism may indeed be dying or dead. However, post Arab spring, an emerging replacement is a modern Pan-Arabism stronger than its predecessor and based on socio-economics on the one hand and Arab secularism on the other. Furthermore, in as much as traditional Pan-Arabism was opposed by the powers, modern Pan-Arabism will be welcomed—indeed encouraged— by those very powers.

Historically, Pan Arab sentiment existed for centuries—I say sentiment because under centuries of Ottoman rule, it was more of a historical reminiscence of Arab Empire than any political fact. In the middle of the last century, it would become institutionalized through the establishment of the Arab League, which would rise to new heights when Egypt's Jamal Abdel Nasser fused Egypt, Syria, and Yemen under one polity, the United Arab Republic. An ambitious project by a charismatic Arab leader, Nasser's revolution combined political reformation with social redress against an Egyptian monarchy that had kept the nation poor and ignorant. Unfortunately, geopolitics would eventually dominate Nasser's agenda. The Suez crisis followed by the war of 1967 would transform his revolution into anti-imperial military rejectionism. Socio-economics took back stage. Upon his passing, several Arab leaders took up his Pan Arab banner with its military rejectionist pole—be it to protest Israel's occupation of Palestinian territory, war against Iran, or the American occupation of Iraq. The socio-economic pole, however, was left by the way side. For the next five decades, while succeeding in selling Pan-Arabism under a military veil, most of the Arab leaders—Saddam, Mubarak, Assad, Ben Ali, and Saleh—all failed in their socio-economic policies. And yet last year, one by one, they were thrown out by the masses (except for Saddam). This tends to suggest that traditional Pan-Arabism with its political and military manifestation no longer sold the Arab masses. They had finally seen through the veil.

But has Pan-Arabism died as a result of the Arab Spring? For the most part, most of the deposed leaders were replaced by democratically elected moderates, which are neither rejectionists nor militaristic. Iraq's governments since Saddam have not been beating the drums of war—rather trying to cope with internal insecurity. Mubarak's replacement is actually in a political battle with the military junta itself. Tunisia's is a Western educated Islamist who has not been preaching war or anti-imperialism. Libya's interim government has also distanced itself from its militarist past under Gaddafi. Interestingly, almost all have been embracing socio-economic reform and as a result a new form of cooperation. After decades of rejecting a common North African market, Libya called for one a mere few weeks after the Gaddafi's death. The GCC is in a serious discussion to speed up monetary union to appease the masses and curb the socio-economic pitfalls. A common Arab customs market is expected by 2020, and which if anything may be moved up. In other arenas and due to technological advances—such as communications, media, and the Internet—integration has already occurred spanning Arab nations on two continents. If anything, all this tends to suggest that a modern Pan-Arabism is thriving.

Some may still argue that the great powers fear and reject Pan-Arabism. They could be right if they are referring to traditional Pan-Arabism. However, the new realities are different today; and it may indeed be in the interest of those powers to see more of modern Pan-Arabism than less of it. This is primarily due to two reasons. First is the massive socio-economic dark cloud hanging over the region, which desperately requires more integration of markets, labor mobility, and fluid direct investment in order to alleviate massive impending economic challenges. The West knows very well that left unattended to its woes it could easily spill into their own backyards—be it in Europe or the United States. Secondly and equally important for the West is the fearful wave of fundamentalism, which many have come to realize is the result of years of regional mismanagement. A modern manifestation of Pan-Arabism could counter the most extremist religious strands and be more secularly inclusive of minorities. The Pan Arab face-off with hardline Syria is an example of such a manifestation. So are Egypt's and Tunisia's constitutional reforms, both of which emphasized the protection of Christian and gender minorities as equal citizens under the law confirming a broad Pan Arab identity without threatening national sovereignty.

Traditional Pan-Arabism as practiced for decades may indeed be dead or dying. This, however, does not mean a modern replacement has not been emerging. Indeed, a stronger strand of Pan-Arabism based on common socio-economic interests and technological links; with institutional steps taken towards free markets, customs unions, labor exchange and direct investment—none of which threaten national sovereignty—seems imminent. Democratizing Arab nations as well as Western powers are quickly reaching the conclusion that it is not only a realization, but perhaps the ultimate salvation. Traditional Pan-Arabism may be dead. Modern Pan-Arabism is just beginning.

SECTION FIVE:
THE EXPAT ROLE IN LEBANON AND THE ARAB WORLD
(2012)

SECTION FIVE:
THE EXPAT ROLE IN LEBANON AND THE ARAB WORLD (2012)

I n the fall of 2012, a new electoral law was presented by the Lebanese government for parliament's ratification. Part of this draft law touched on the voting rights of Lebanese expatriates. It was basically the first time in the nation's history that this issue was being seriously tackled and that Lebanese expatriates were potentially being given a full voice in how their homeland was being run.

Having left Lebanon almost twenty five years earlier and now firmly an expatriate myself, I found this subject close to my heart. After all, my grandfather had been a Lebanese expat in India, my father had been one in Europe and the Middle East, and my son was now following in all our footsteps in the United States and South America. So, I delved into studying the issue and closely monitoring the debate back in the homeland. Unfortunately, I quickly began finding anomalies and contradictions.

For instance, I found that the predecessor 2008 election law, while recognizing the Lebanese expat voting rights, was functionally almost impossible to implement. It essentially boxed expats into the same broken political system that the Lebanese had been suffering from for the past half century, forcing them to vote for the same sectarian local districts where they did not live. Indeed, many expats around the world had no direct contact with or consequence from district politics or representatives in which they were being asked to register to vote; and yet the election law of 2008 seemed completely oblivious to it. As if that were not enough, the law forced expats to pre-register to vote—something which local inhabitants in Lebanon did not need to do. It placed an even higher barrier by forcing each expat jurisdiction to have at least 200 registered voters to even qualify for a ballot box. Of course, each expat jurisdiction was not defined by the foreign location or country of residence, rather by the total expats in that jurisdiction that pertained to a single district in Lebanon! So, practically if you had five hundred people registering in say Paris, 199 of which came from Beirut, 150 from Tripoli, and 151 from Mount Lebanon; none of them would get to vote because none of the expat jurisdictions reached the minimum ballot benchmark of 200. Functionally, this meant few if any expats would actually get to vote even if they had registered. As a result, many expats would eventually feel slighted once they realized the whole exercise had been a waste of their time.

The 2012 draft law, however, in its expat component was a definite improvement. It basically suggested dedicating six new members of parliament to be voted for exclusively by expats around the world and did not have any minimum benchmarks pertaining to local Lebanese districts. The law was more grounded in that it guaranteed voting for the expats and proper representation by members of parliament from their own global communities. Moreover, for the first time in Lebanese history, this group of MPs would be chosen in a completely nonsectarian way—albeit abiding by the 50% Christian-Moslem ratio in line with Lebanon's constitution. I found this to be a hugely positive reform step for the nation that almost no one was highlighting in any of the debates.

Unfortunately, the 2012 law was never promoted enough by the government that had submitted it, nor was it ever ratified by parliament having been ball-chained to a controversial larger election-law reform package that had little to do with expats. But what surprised me the most was to see so many people in Lebanon outright rejecting the idea of expat MPs without really understanding it, preferring instead to have the expats vote for the incumbent 128 MP slots in parliament. By doing so, they unwittingly diluted the expat vote to such a degree so as to dis-incentivize expats from even registering to vote. And indeed few expats even registered under the de facto law of 2008—barely 10,000 actually registered from supposedly millions residing abroad! As a sampling, in my own district of Mina in Tripoli (in which I've never really lived), out of some 29,000 local registrations, I counted only 102 expats, including close friends and family whom I had lobbied, all amounting to less than 0.36% of the total registered constituency. To add insult to injury, they came from as far afield as Australia, America, and Europe meaning none of us would eventually be able to vote as none of our global jurisdictions reached the 200-minimum requirement in our district. I would venture to say that nowhere in the world does the Mina district have a concentration of 200 potential voters. Many regions in Lebanon suffered from the same problem. This meant whoever designed the 2008 law was either being disingenuous with the expats or had overlooked a major flaw.

Come registration time, the government had barely any resources or budget to mobilize expat registrations. To be fair, the Lebanese diplomatic community, including ambassadors and consuls, who were tasked with promoting expat voter registrations tried their best. Unfortunately, in private, Lebanese diplomats I conversed with complained of limited budgets and limited staff. One official confided that he barely had a budget to pay regular staff salaries, let alone hire new staff to promote expat registration.

Civil groups did not fare much better. Even progressive Lebanese groups were pretty stuck to the erroneous notion that Members of Parliament need to be local and expats need to vote for them just like everyone else. They were unwilling to consider the representatives that the expats were asking for. One local gentleman I met in Beirut asked me, "How do I make sure an expat member of parliament responds to my needs?" to which I responded somewhat mystified, "Shouldn't you first be worried about holding accountable your local district politician and the incumbent 128 local MPs?!"

On reflection, the gentleman's question, while seemingly ironic, showed either that local Lebanese society had given up against the unaccountable domination of their local parliamentarian representatives; or they were expecting the expats to solve the problem for them by voting in better representatives. Little did they know that the expats were as disinterested in delving into petty local politics as they were in voting under the same old system, which had led the nation to a social, economic, and political cliff.

Another rather silly local argument that I came across was the cost of the six new expat members of parliament to the government's coffers. With national debt soaring up to around sixty billion dollars, the argument that an additional $600,000 per year spend to engage the expats more effectively would suddenly break the bank seemed too ludicrous to respond to. It certainly didn't convince expats who provide more or less 20% of GDP remittances, totaling almost $10 billion annually.

What I found most tragic in the whole expat law mishap was that most of the voices being heard were those of local Lebanese who wanted to involve their expat compatriots; but not necessarily hear what they had to say. Out of the many debates on satellite television, only one was conducted abroad with actual expats. The rest were all local with local politicians voicing what they thought the role of the expats should be. The expats were pretty much limited to the occasional dial-in.

All of the above eventually caused the expats to simply lose interest, perhaps intuitively understanding the futility of the whole exercise. So, I resolved to widen the scope of the conversation by launching a social media group, which would essentially bring together Lebanese expat communities from all over the world to voice their opinions. The Facebook group, Lebanese Expats for a Better Homeland, essentially became a community of global expat communities spanning the globe from Australia to Europe to North and South America. The idea was to generate more opinions and get people to think about the issues and what they really meant.

One of the most interesting byproducts of this community was an Expat Strategy Paper, which was published in December 2012 and shared worldwide. The goal of the paper was to strip the issue of Lebanese expats to its bare elements, objectively study the issue outside of local political calculations, and make some actionable recommendations going forward. My hope was that it would serve Lebanon and the Arab world by presenting new ideas of how these societies could tap their highly educated and productive expatriate communities living all over the world. The goal of course would be to advance the emerging democracies and create desperately needed economic nexus.

The Nature of the Lebanese Expatriate Issue (December 2012)

Lebanon has been a nation of immigrants throughout its history. In good times and in bad, in ancient times and in modern, the Lebanese have left their homeland as their ancestors before them. In the past, however, immigrants often lost touch with their homeland because of lack of communication and ease of travel. As a result, for centuries Lebanon had been losing touch with its immigrating sons and daughters. This loss implied a brain drain with direct economic and social implications on the nation, which Lebanon had few means to combat let alone overcome.

The modern age, however, has changed how Diasporas all over the world are seen by their home nations, and how they themselves see their homelands. Easy travel has been accompanied with technological advances allowing homelands and their respective expatriates to be more engaged through constant technological contact. Lebanon has been no exception. In fact, faced with mounting internal problems, the country increasingly sees hope in the Lebanese expatriate community, as a resource to count on. "Our expats are more valuable than some other countries' oil" one analyst put it. And many consider this resource to have become an irreplaceable pillar for the nation. It is not hard to see why:

Almost 22% of the nation's GDP is derived from expat remittances (approximately USD $8.4 billion in 2010, according to the World Bank). This figure, however, does not take into consideration several other benefits. First, it does not take into account the hundreds of thousands of Lebanese expats visiting their homeland annually and spending locally, helping elevate tourism revenue, which the nation direly counts on *(Bank Audi Research Report, Q3, 2012)*. Second, it does not consider the billions of expat deposits already in Lebanon's banks and which form a large percentage of Lebanese bank's $150 billion in deposits *(Bank Audi Research Report, Q3, 2012)*. This generates significant trickle-down effects on the homeland's local economy. Thirdly, it does not measure the impact of service exports to expat communities. For instance, by tapping expats communities all over the world, Lebanese satellite TV generates revenue for the nation. And finally, it does not consider the massive economic benefits derived from network externalities generated from the Lebanon's connections with its communities worldwide. This not only has provided a constant flow of ideas, opportunities, and exports; but effectively has kept Lebanon on the map, particularly during the nation's darkest hours. It should all come as no surprise, therefore, that Lebanon is seeking to find ways to engage more effectively with its expat community.

As it happens, with the global information and technology revolution, the Lebanese expats themselves feel ever more connected with their homeland. A lot of them are up to speed through satellite TV and the Internet. They travel more often and communicate more frequently via a multitude of technological tools. They are also looking for ways to engage with Lebanon more permanently and effectively to further their interests as well. They see opportunities not only inside Lebanon, but as importantly through this homeland to regional markets. Therefore, while emotional attachment to the homeland is certainly one driver, hard interests are increasingly playing a role to the expats.

It is the intersection of the interests of Lebanon and those of its expats, which has the potential for creating an enduring link, with massive potential benefits to all. This intersection in the past has been primarily informal and based on individual initiative. It has worked to a certain degree as the aforementioned economic numbers clearly show. But the question the government is now asking is what more potential could exist if some of the channels between the Lebanese expatriate community and their homeland could be strengthened through some sort of institutionalized representation?

Defining What the Expat Issue is About (December 2012)

Before attempting to establish enduring strategies and make proper policy recommendations, it is crucially important to understand how best to define the Lebanese expat issue. We can begin doing this by dispelling four common misconceptions:

It's about the Homeland but it's also about the Expats: The first major misconception is that the expat issue is solely about how the expats will be helping Lebanon. While this is certainly a goal that many hope to achieve, it is only part of the story. One must not forget the other side of the equation—how the homeland can help the expats. Indeed, the first should be seen as an emotional invitation to help, but unfortunately this in itself has time and again proven to be a weak incentive. Considering how Lebanon may also be able to help the expats provides a stronger and more enduring incentive with tangibly hard to refute economic benefits—something which it is reasonable to expect would garner a more effective and lasting type of engagement. Here's a simple example to prove the point:

Not long ago, Lebanon launched an initiative to help reduce the mounting national debt by asking its expats to help out. It did so by asking them to donate directly to the state coffers. International bank account details were advertised in different media outlets in Lebanon and all over the world on satellite television and the Internet. The hope of course was that the expats would feel compelled to help their homeland. So essentially, it was an emotional call with no direct benefits to the expats except that of feeling good to help their homeland. Unfortunately, the results proved to be pathetic, and preliminary reports showed that there were merely a few thousand dollars received. The plan was soon shelved and never heard of again. Now let's contrast this to the billions of dollars sent every year into Lebanese banks by the expatriate community. Because interest rates are higher, essentially expats have been incentivized to repatriate some of their money to the homeland. According to the Lebanese Bank Association, it is estimated that there are more than $20 billion expat deposits in Lebanese banks. Such a policy has lasted for more than 20 years and has been very successful because it is derived from hard interests serving both the nation through the strengthening of its banking sector as well as the expats who received good interest payments on their deposits.

The positive element of this type of a policy is that it benefits Lebanon and the expatriates simultaneously. It is also one of the key reasons why the banking sector in Lebanon continues to defy all political crises—its deposits do not depend solely on the local market. One can only imagine how many other ideas could generate similar positive dynamics with similarly positive effects for the nation and its expats.

It's about Progressive Policies not Backward-looking Calculations:
The second common misconception has to do with expat political inclinations. Whether through unscrupulous behavior or desperate measure, there are some leaders in Lebanon who are trying to turn the issue of Lebanon's expats into a sectarian balancing act of sorts. The assumption here is that a lot of the expats have been of a certain religious denomination; and if they are brought back to vote, then they would counter-balance the opposing growing local denominations. This calculation is as politically misguided as it is futile. Most expats at one point or another decided to leave their homeland because of some of these very restricting calculations that had placed glass ceilings over their futures. To be asked after all these years to further these divisive policies is as foolhardy as it is naïve.

Expats in their foreign habitats are not sectarian in nature. If that were purely the case, then one would not have seen as many Lebanese Christians in the Muslim Gulf countries nor as many Lebanese Muslims as abundantly in the Christian West. In fact, in some nations descendants of a certain denomination with time have even changed their religion—as has been documented in Argentina for instance. The truth is, Lebanese expats have had plenty of time to amalgamate into new polities, few of which have the type of religious segregation found inside of Lebanon. As a result, expats are likely to prove to be more progressively secular and issue-orientated in their voting than many in Lebanon expect.

Perhaps the biggest proof is the recent ridiculously low voter registration rates of the expats. If for instance, some of Lebanon's immigrants maintained the sectarian existential fears that persist in Lebanon, then the percentage of those registering to vote would naturally have been much higher—especially since this is the first time in history that they can vote. The alleged existential fears they have would have been a good motivator. But it wasn't, and expats did not register as expected. In other words, they do not garner the same fears or boxed-in-sectarian calculations that their brethren back in the homeland have been duped into believing all these years. Religious imbalance concern is something that affects acute local Lebanese politicians and does nothing to further the cause of Lebanese expats.

It's about National Issues not Local Politics: Thirdly, the false notion that expats should get involved in local politics is a fundamentally flawed concept. Sure, expats hear the news—the national news at least—and may read about this or that occurrence; but when it comes to the daily grind of purely local issues (for example what happens in this or that town, a school built in this or that district, security in a specific neighborhood …), most will have little knowledge or be affected by them. Indeed, forcing expat involvement at the micro local level arguably may have negative repercussions. This can be exemplified as per the following:

Let's consider a case scenario where we have a village whose mayor has offered to build either a new school or alternatively a large summer swimming facility. Now let's assume the local Lebanese living in the town prefer to have a school for their children. But they are out-funded by the wealthier expats lobbying for a summer swimming facility since. As unfair as it may seem, expats may see no immediate benefit to themselves or their families living abroad in building the school. Now, assuming the town has limited resources, and cannot fund both projects, the net result could end up being a large pool serving the town's expats a few weeks of the year, but no school. This may seem to some as an unlikely scenario, but many argue that Lebanese cabinets in the mid to late 1990's did just this by overly focusing on rebuilding Beirut in order to attract Lebanon's wealthy expats and Arabs. Unfortunately, with limited resources, ultimately this policy came at the expense of the local Lebanese whose regions fell behind becoming dilapidated. Whether or not this over-simplification has merit, in the very least, it does raise a valid question as to what level expat involvement should be and for what purpose.

Ideally, expat involvement and representation need to be at a level where policies carry a consequence on the respective expat community, and not micro locally where in all likelihood it wouldn't. This should not be translated into an attempt to push expats out of the local decision making. Rather, expats who would like to be involved locally should be allowed to establish local residency in said constituency, thus assuring the link between vote and consequence. To this we turn to in the final point.

It's about Understanding Expat Characteristics and Applying Proper Laws and Policies: It is important to understand that the notion that expats are a rigidly constructed group is yet another fallacy. An expat today may decide to return to Lebanon tomorrow. Similarly, a Lebanese resident today may become an expat in the future. This fluidity is very likely to increase as the world continues to globalize and interconnect. A parallel point to keep in mind is that expats are not all alike. Further on, we discuss in detail the different types of expat profiles and their specific—sometimes conflicting—needs. Suffice it to say here that a policy targeting the "Working Expat" may not work on the "Long-term Expat" any more than it would on a fourth generation "Descendant Expat". When dealing with Lebanon's expats, careful analysis of nuance and application of commensurate policies are keys to success.

A good example to clarify this point would be the election law passed in 2008. In its expat component, it essentially lumped all types of expats into one large bucket, asking them to vote for an MP in the local Lebanese district of their forefathers. At face value, this may seem like a reasonable policy meant to give expats a voice. However, if one analyzes the types of expats, and specifically in looking at two large categories of expats, one will find that the "Long-term Expat" category, which no longer enjoys close links to Lebanon, would find a vote for a local district member of parliament rather irrelevant and of little consequence. Proof of this has been the very low voter registration rates, particularly in countries where the mass of "long-term" immigrants reside—namely the United States, Brazil, and Mexico—none of which even made the voter registration benchmark. On the other hand, if this law was meant to attract the "Working Expats" who may live close to Lebanon (the Gulf countries), these expats generally spend their summers in Lebanon escaping the gulf heat anyway, so it wouldn't attract them to register abroad either because they would just vote in Lebanon that very summer. And since "Descendant Expats" for all intents and purposes are too far genealogically to trace their roots, the 2008 law wasn't going to do that much to this category to begin with. So of what use was that law? Is it a wonder then that only 10,000 out of hundreds of thousands—not to say millions—globally ended up registering? Unfortunately, this very general law of 2008, while a good first step, did not attempt to understand the expat nuances enough to apply the proper policy commensurate to attracting them to register to vote. (Some would argue that considering the deficiency in the law and in its application, reaching 10,000 registrants was actually not bad at all).

In conclusion, the Lebanese expat issue is about Lebanon but as importantly also about the expats; it's about progressive policies not backward-looking acute calculations; it's about national issues not local politics; and it's about understanding expat characteristics and applying proper laws and policies.

Defining the Different Lebanese Expat Categories (December 2012)

Before we begin defining the different Lebanese expat categories, let us first establish and accept a fact of life: Immigration in Lebanon is inevitable. It is part of Lebanon's past, present, and will be a part of its future. Indeed, with an increasingly interconnected world, this trend is likely to increase not decrease, because Lebanon's educated young as much as they may love their homeland are now connected with the world at large in ways that will induce them to reach higher and further than what their homeland can ever offer on its own. This, however, should not be seen as a deficiency; for much larger and prosperous nations such as England, Italy, Spain, and Germany have all managed to prosper notwithstanding the tens of millions leaving their homelands. Some nations, such as Israel and Ireland actually argue that part of their prosperity is owed to a continuous cycle of immigration. The historical cases of Britain and Spain are indisputable and came as a result of their large expatriate activity over several centuries (the British in North America and the Spaniards in South America).

The area that is now Lebanon itself felt the power of this kind of network externality in the days of the Phoenicians who through sea-faring commercialism managed to colonize large swathes of the Mediterranean basin and become one of the most prosperous ancient civilizations in the area. Of course, if we are willing to accept the fact that Lebanon will always be an immigrant nation and its borders simply too small to support the ambition of its people, then the next step would be to embrace immigration's positive elements and start thinking about dealing with its implications. To do this, we must start by understanding the different types of Lebanese expatriates and how they can be engaged. Here we find three categories of expats:

Type I—The Working Expat: The first type is a "Working Expat" with strong connections to the homeland and frequent visits. Sometimes the nucleus of the family is split with one "Working Expat" spouse living abroad and the other in Lebanon. Included in this type are also temporary Lebanese students who may be studying overseas but whose families are still in Lebanon; or temporary workers of Lebanese companies working a multi-year assignment somewhere but who plan to return to Lebanon in the near term. For all these Type I "Working Expats", what goes on locally in Lebanon and specifically in their respective district of residence (or plan to reside upon return) is of importance and of direct consequence to themselves and their families. Ironically, this dynamic also makes this expat type the least that the government of Lebanon may be interested in engaging, because essentially they are already highly engaged. These are the expats who already frequently visit Lebanon, own real estate, own bank accounts, spend locally (especially if part of the nucleus of the family still lives in Lebanon), and consume heavily taxed items such as gasoline, mobile telephony, etc. ... From a practical perspective, it is unlikely that these types of expats could be any more heavily engaged than they already are whether they get to vote abroad or not. Besides, the interests of many of these expats are likely to be much more associated with Lebanon proper and their own district than a temporary expat jurisdiction, which they will likely leave sooner rather than later. More on this further on.

Type II—The Long-term Expat: This is the second category and can be defined as anyone who may have been born in Lebanon or is a close 2nd generation, with reasonably good connections to the homeland as well as occasional visitation. This type of expat, however, left the homeland years ago and has created a geographically distant home, which he does not intend to leave in the near future. And while they may never return to live in the homeland and are not directly affected by its day-to-day, they generally care about Lebanon and its future. What happens inside of a certain district in Lebanon (a school, a bridge, a water pipe, utilities...) does not have a direct consequence on the life of this type of expat. But because of their longevity abroad, this type of expat is the very one who has the most resources to help the homeland. In other words, this is precisely the type of expat the Lebanese government is desperately hoping to tap. Not only do they have resources and connections all over the world that could highly benefit the nation, but they have rarely been tapped in any institutional way.

Unfortunately, the very same longevity of these "Long-term Expats" (particularly those in North and South America, Europe, and Australia) has made them part and parcel of well-functioning democracies. They understand voting, they understand representation, and they understand accountability. Many are not very impressed with post-war Lebanon's political development and voice concern over their lack of representation. Indeed, the closest they have come to any semblance of representation are the diplomatic missions (embassies and consulates), whose missions are traditionally more government-to-government than government-to-expats. The good news is that the Lebanese government seems to have realized this deficiency and the dire need to engage this specific type of expat in fundamentally different ways. The election law of 2008, however, has fallen short and done little to sway this crucial group. Many have come to see the government's efforts as a mediocre attempt to alter the dynamics of an existing chasm with the homeland; not meriting even registration to vote in the Lebanese embassies.

To be swayed, this type of expat will need properly thought out policies that have hard incentives and representation, justifying engagement. Haphazard laws and acutely local policies are not the way to do it and will continue to fail. To this effect, this type of expat is not that interested in confessionalism or gerrymandering. They live in environments that shield them to a certain degree from such thinking and instead allow them to focus on larger national goals and their own long-term interests. Therefore, they are likely to be more interested in seeing progressive policies and laws involving hard interests that have direct implication on them, while positively helping

Lebanon at the national level, not necessarily the district level. Anything less than that will be perceived as a waste of their time.

Type III—The Descendant Expat: At the other end of the expat spectrum, we find what I would term the "Descendant Expat," who for all intents and purposes knows of a Lebanon—and may even garner sympathy to the "ancestral homeland"—but in reality no longer has any direct links with it at all—be it familiar, social, economic or political. For these expats, Lebanon is a spirit in a similar vein as French Canadians may feel to France, Aussies to Britain, and Mexicans to Spain. But any immediate links may have been severed a long time ago. In Argentina for instance, a large part of the Lebanese community finds it difficult to trace their ancestry because upon entry to Argentina, the names of their ancestors were altered by either immigration authorities or the church, in order to streamline the immigration process. Engaging these types of expats presents legal difficulties; the kind of which are by no means insurmountable, but practically the government at this point does not have the capabilities, resources, or time to overcome. Nevertheless, these Lebanese expats could be attended to in innovative ways in the future, but immediate focus should be placed on the first two expat types.

In conclusion, Lebanon needs to understand that there are three major types of expats, each of which has peculiarities and implications that demand carefully thought-out laws and policies. Having one-size fits policies will continue to fail as many have so far.

A Deeper Look at Lebanon's Expat Numbers (December 2012)

In Lebanon, the topic of expat numbers often generates debate, with numbers varying from the hundreds of thousands to the tens of millions. To avoid unnecessary subjectivity, let us for the time being stick to numbers that well-respected global NGOs commonly use. According to the World Bank, for instance, Lebanon's recorded expats in 2010 numbered approximately 664,000 (source: Peoplemov.in, World Bank, Bilateral Migration and Remittances 2010, Migration and Remittances Fact book 2011). Of course, this is way below the millions and probably discounts many who may not be recorded or who may have left Lebanon even before the recording began. For argument's sake let us stick to this figure, which comes out to more or less 16% of the total Lebanese population. Also according to the World Bank, expat remittances for 2010 amounted close to $8.4 billion, which is about 22% of Lebanon's GDP. If we look at the banking sector, according to the Association of Lebanese Banks for 2010, the non-resident deposits in Lebanese banks amounted to about $27 billion out of a total of $140 billion, which is about 19%. So for all intents and purposes, the quantity of active Lebanese expats estimated by the World Bank seems to be aligned with the corresponding percentage of the economy in remittances as well as with the deposits, and is more or less 20%. That is not to say there aren't any expats who have not been recorded, or that there are those who do not send remittances, or those who have not made deposits. It is simply a statistical average based on World Bank statistics.

What does this all mean to expat representation? Assuming we take this low average number of 20%, let us then proceed to value the expats themselves in proportion to Lebanon, and in so doing try to estimate what would merit a fair democratic representation—focusing particularly on the national parliament at this point. If for example, we base representation on population, and assuming all citizens should have an equal representation, then Lebanon's parliament of 128 members should logically have 20 parliamentarian representing the diaspora (128×16%= 20.48). This means, 108 would be representatives from districts within Lebanon and 20 representing the expat districts. If we did the same exercise based on % of GDP, then the number of expat representatives should actually go up to 28. In other words, 100 MPs representing the local districts and 28 representing the expat districts. And if we consider deposits, it would be somewhere in the middle.

Some may argue that there should be no such thing as an expat district and that expats should vote for the 128 MP slots like everyone else. They argue that by having an average of 20% representation, in reality it is taking away 100% of the right to vote for any representative in parliament. This logic is a fallacy, because the primary assumption it makes is that expat interests match those of the local population in terms of constituency and representative needs, which we have already shown above that it doesn't. Even worse, by forcing expats to vote for local representatives, it automatically dilutes the expat vote by a factor of 5 in favor of the local voters because on average for every expat voter voting for a local representative, there will inevitably be 4 local voters. Therefore the odds of having a representative serving expat interests (which also serve Lebanon) not only becomes lower, but they are so globally dispersed that the candidate representative him or herself has little incentive to invest to acquire this expat voter (after all it is much simpler, cheaper, and quantitatively more effective to go after the local voter). This is precisely why local MPs quite rationally do not waste their time or resources travelling the world for meager expat votes. So essentially by promising expats 128 MPs instead of a guaranteed amount of say 20 representatives from within their midst, it is not unlike selling a lottery ticket whose jackpot is huge, but whose probability of winning is so remote as to dis-incentivize most of the population from buying it. Just because I can vote for 128 MPs, it doesn't mean that I can influence the decisions of any of them. This is one of the fundamental reasons for why so few Lebanese expats actually registered to vote for Lebanon's parliament.

This dynamic is bound to change if expats are given their own fair contingency within the Lebanese parliament—one which can make a positive impact on their own lives as well as that of their homeland, unchained to acute sectarian or micro-local agendas. The pending draft law of 2012 took this into account by proposing a contingent of 6 MPs for the sole purpose of representing the expats. And even though the 6 MPs as a number are decidedly lower than even the low expat population percentage of total estimates (16%), the law would in the very least guarantee that there would be some degree of dedicated representation.

The Economic Potential of Smarter Expat Engagement (December 2012)

One of the most similar Diasporas in dimension and influence around the world is the Israeli, which according to the World Bank in 2010 was estimated at around 700,000. In comparing it with Lebanon's diaspora, what is different between both groups is that in Lebanon, immigration is seen as negative. In Israel, however, it is increasingly seen as inevitable with positive elements. While subtle, the difference is actually significant in the application of policy. For instance, the Israelis have now understood that there is no way Israel as a nation could absorb its tens of thousands of highly trained expats in North America and Europe. Instead of giving up on the issue, they have fostered what they term circular migration:

"According to demographer Pini Herman, this circular migration has been an economic boon to Israel. Israel does not have the technological, academic, and other infrastructural resources to absorb its disproportionate number of highly trained and skilled population, second only to the United States. As a result, many Israelis have worked overseas for extended periods of time. Upon their return, they have often attracted or repatriated with them to Israel new infrastructure, such as that provided by companies like Intel, Google, Microsoft, and IBM."

Stop Worrying about Yordim,
The Jewish Forward, 2012.
Also, Circular Migration in Israel, Robert Shuman
Center for Advanced Studies, Florence, Italy

This poses two key questions: First, how could migration be turned into a positive phenomenon that helps a homeland? And second, how can one measure its potential impact on an emigrant country like Lebanon?

The answer to the first question is: migration could be turned into a positive phenomenon due to network externalities. Network externality is an economic term that describes a disproportionate rise in value due to some type of economic connectivity. A typical example is that of a telephone network: Having one phone connected to another brings the potential of making one call from phone A to phone B, and one from phone B back to phone A. Adding two other connections (phones C and D) to the first two would not double but sextuple the possibilities as it now allows for TWELVE possible connections: A to B, B to A, A to C, C to A, A to D, D to A, B to C, C to B, B to D, D to B, C to D, and D to C. Network externalities are all about expanding networks, which create new economic possibilities and hence value or wealth. Every immigrant from Lebanon by default establishes a new connection. And every connection potentially brings new avenues of opportunity and wealth. The Phoenicians internalized this phenomenon three millennia ago and colonized the entire Mediterranean basin, prospering as a result. The Dutch and British did it for centuries and built vast amounts of wealth. Israel is applying a similar principal. Modern day Lebanon should embrace this phenomenon as well and work on harnessing its benefits.

This brings us to the second question: What is the estimated value a well-tapped Diaspora could potentially bring to Lebanon? Quantitatively, this question is not easy to answer and the statistics are not detailed enough to allow us to have a definitive answer. But we could utilize two relatively simple models to estimate the potential effects of engaging expats more effectively. The first model essentially would estimate reaching more expats through more structured engagement and realizing value as a result. For instance, if Lebanon could double the amount of expats it can reach, then the potential remittances could possibly double, so would tourism and perhaps expat deposits. This means a net economic amount reaching anywhere between $8 billion and $15 billion per year. This model is fundamentally weak because it is based on the assumption that the 660,000 or so World Bank reported Lebanese expats are not already highly engaged. And yet on average, Lebanon receives some $12,000 per expat per year ($8 billion in remittances divided by 660,000 expats), which is already relatively very high by any standard. Comparatively, for instance, the United Kingdom's equivalent of remittance per expat per year is only $1,797, Italy's is just $2,121, and the Israel's is just $1,446. As it stands, in fact, Lebanon ranks as the 8th highest in the world in the world, and percentage wise, the absolute highest in middle and high income nations, according to the World Bank's 2011 Remittances Data Inflow report.

This either points to a national statistical anomaly or all these nations actually managed to engage their expats differently empowering network externalities, which ended up having a more powerful economic influence on the local GDP than purely from remittances. For example, network externalities through smart policies such as "Israel's circular migration" policy attracting Israeli researchers and workers from top technology companies all over the world would hardly make a dent on remittances; but what it does do is boost the local economy by creating connections between expat scientific communities, global client companies, and local Israeli high tech startups. Numbers can help shed some more light on this. In 2011, for instance, Israel's economy while $242.9 billion only reported $1.5 billion in remittances. This means that Israel as opposed to asking its expats to send remittances (a weak form of expat support), actually was promoting policies for them to invest in or continuously network local companies with the world. This provided the local economy with technology, innovation, and sustained growth while providing expat Israeli investors with a high rate of return (a strong and enduring form of expat support). In the process, Israel managed to see industries such as defense, security, and information technology all become highly developed. Arguably, the only such industry that has managed to do some of this in Lebanon is banking, which was born with policies supporting a global view. Unfortunately, banking as an industry traditionally does not provide an economy with as much long-term upside as say technology.

Coming back to the case of Israel, network externalities through a policy of circular migration appears to have positively fed into the nation's growth, and provided it with an economy 6 times the size of Lebanon's even though Israel receives a fifth of Lebanon's remittances. Quantitatively, from this perspective, and if we take into account the difference in population size (Israel has double the population as Lebanon and has a commensurate level of education), the net effect of network externalities could potentially amount to more or less a triplication of the local economy. In other words, Lebanon has the potential of growing from a $34 billion local economy (net of the $8 billion in annual remittances) to a $100 billion potential economy.

As has been shown above, because of the massive potential economic effects, it is imperative to elevate the expat issue to the top of the national agenda and keep it there together with other equally important national issues.

Making the Case for Expat Members of Parliament (December 2012)

Over the past century, and notwithstanding wave after another of immigration, local members of parliament have proven themselves to be preoccupied with fundamentally local issues and inattentive to expat needs. Even after the passage of the 2008 expat voting law, local MPs rationally saw that a diluted expat vote is not worth their time or investment; and very few exerted any worthwhile effort to lobby the expat communities over the subsequent 5 years. Therefore, if Lebanon is truly interested in engaging its expats to tap into the massive economic potential, the only way to do it appears to be through dedicated expat MPs who are first responsive to the needs of their expat constituencies. And second, these expat MPs need to focus on the establishment and growth of global economic networks, serving both their constituency as well as the homeland as a whole. Such expat MPs will prove to be more valuable and more worthy of a vote for the Lebanese expats than any other local Lebanese MP because they will provide their respective expat constituency with the needed level of:

1) Understanding
2) Responsiveness
3) Representation

It is equally imperative that expat MPs be linked to the geography they represent so as to be held accountable by their constituencies for their work and results. It would do no one any good to have expat MPs on one side of the globe representing an important expat community on the other. This will be discussed in more detail later on.

Issues Expat MPs Would Need to Support and Promote (December 2012)

Expat issues need to be framed in such a way where synergies could be found between how expats can help Lebanon and, as stated prior, in how Lebanon can help its expats. In other words there needs to be a concerted and flowing balance between the two. Some policies and programs that expats may be keen to see implemented in the homeland for the mutual benefit of Lebanon and the Lebanese expat community include:

A Sampling of Expat Constituency Issues	Helps Lebanon	Helps Constituency
Investment and trade opportunities in Lebanon	✓	✓
Jobs and internships in Lebanon for constituency and for Lebanese youth abroad	✓	✓
Expat business opportunities and links in and through Lebanon	✓	✓
Lebanese export opportunities in expat constituencies	✓	✓
Banking and finance bridges to Lebanon from constituencies	✓	✓
Direct air bridges to and from expat constituency	✓	✓
Tourism and cultural exchange to Lebanon	✓	✓
Educational links from Lebanon to expat constituencies	✓	✓
Automation of voter registration and unencumbered transfer between local and expat constituencies	✓	✓
Adoption of Lebanese orphans by Lebanese expats	✓	✓
Tracing roots and nationality Laws for expat spouses, children	✓	✓

Of course, there are some purely national issues that expats may be just as keen. In such cases, they should be treated as any other represented district constituency, voicing its concern within the overall parliament. Some of these issues may include progressive agenda items such as:

A Sampling of National Issues	Helps Lebanon	Helps Expats
Constitutional amendment for equal rights among all Lebanese citizens including the expats	✓	✓
Full women's rights on all issues including civil marriage, citizenship, inheritance, ... etc.	✓	✓
Fair economic distribution and development to those areas most in need	✓	✓
Accelerated government decentralization and accountability	✓	✓
IT policies and Internet connectivity	✓	✓
Banking laws and taxation policies	✓	✓
A sound national security and defense	✓	✓
100% education charter to all Lebanese under 18 years of age	✓	✓
Maintaining the environment in Lebanon	✓	✓
National infrastructure (international roads and driving standards)	✓	✓

While expats should be given a voice and a platform when it comes to national issues, as mentioned, this should not be translated into interference with highly local issues, which may fall under non-expat jurisdictions. For instance, a citizen living in Baabda will likely see very little consequence from a school being built in Marjaioun. There is no reason to expect any differently from a Lebanese expat in Melbourne, Australia over something highly local occurring in either Baabda or Marjaioun. Expat priorities are naturally different and their representatives will likely be voted for to push their respective priorities and attain the necessary government concessions to make them a reality. In this sense, and not unlike democracies all over the world, the Lebanese and Lebanese expats should learn to trust one another to push for and vote for their own geographic interests with direct consequence on their respective daily lives. Some may argue that some expats (especially the Type I "Working Expats") would prefer to vote locally because they will soon enough return to that locality. In said case, if an expat would prefer to act locally, there is no reason to deny them that right, and give them the choice to do so, as shall be discussed further below.

In conclusion, expats have issues that pertain specifically to them in their foreign jurisdictions not unlike local jurisdictions inside of Lebanon have their own. Each respective jurisdiction should have a say in its own needs, and should not interfere or influence the others on its own issues. But they should also all come together when it comes to determining the national agenda, as it affects everyone.

What Lebanese Expats Really Want from a New Election Law (December 2012)

In September of 2012, the Lebanese President and cabinet submitted for parliamentary ratification a new election law. A key novelty in this new bill is its expat voting component, which if the law is ratified, essentially means for the first time in Lebanon's history, Lebanese expats all over the world, numbering in the millions, will be allowed to vote for six of their own representatives to become full-fledged Lebanese parliamentarians. These newly introduced expat MP slots are in addition to the 128 incumbent local MP slots. Albeit short of what the expats had been demanding in terms of magnitude of representation, it pointed to a good start. Nevertheless, the law left out some key details.

First, how will these new expat MPs be chosen? In other words, will they be chosen by continent, by hemisphere, or simply by total vote count regardless of geography? From a practical perspective, as mentioned above, it would be more desirable to have expat MPs responsive to the needs of their respective region. For instance, to have an expat MP based in the Arab Gulf trying to service the lobbying needs of a community as far away as Canada or Brazil is impractical and unsustainable. Therefore, it is more effective that the expat MPs be chosen by continent or by hemisphere. Under such a scenario, if the number of MPs as presented in the 2012 draft law is 6 expat MPs, it may be wiser to have some geographic segmentation, an example of which could be 2 expat MPs from the Americas, 2 from Europe and Africa, and 2 from Asia and Australia. The MP should ideally reside in his or her expat constituency and fly to Lebanon whenever parliament is in session legislating—not unlike a congressman from Hawaii does in Washington DC (a 10-hour flight from Honolulu and a 6 hour time-zone difference, commensurate to a flight from say, North America to Lebanon with an equivalent time difference). Suffice it to say, the closer the MP is to their constituency, the better they will be able to service and represent it in the national parliament.

Second, as it pertains to the issue of sectarianism, expats in their foreign habitats are not sectarian in nature, and generally do not act in a sectarian way. As a result, generally speaking expats may prove to be more secularly orientated in their voting. The issue here becomes maintaining the Lebanese constitution's equal Muslim-Christian ratio in parliament. While many expats would prefer not to even consider it, it would perhaps be most suitable to keep this ratio in each of the expat regions for the time being so as not to oppose the constitution. Further sect-specific dissection, however, would not be practical as 6 expat MP slots simply cannot be sliced nor diced into Lebanon's 18 sects. It would be futile and shunned by the expat community. Fortunately, the suggested 2012 law eliminates sectarianism as long as it falls within the 50-50 Christian-Muslim split, with the top 3 of each religion becoming MPs regardless of sect. This should be considered quite progressive in that it is the first election law in Lebanese history to essentially eliminate sectarianism.

Third, what happens if an expat prefers to vote for a local MP and not an expat MP? Will they be given the choice to do so; or would they be obliged to travel back to Lebanon to exercise that option if they so wish? Here, it is important to note the difference between two afore-mentioned large groups of Lebanese expat communities. The first was referred to as "Working Expats" and the second "Long-term Expats". On the one hand, the "Working Expat" typically lives closer to Lebanon and visits frequently (from/to the Arab Gulf, for example). As stated this type of expat is naturally engaged with local issues and for good reason—the local school, road, and government may directly affect them and their families. Therefore, voting carries an immediate consequence to them and their families inside of Lebanon, for which reason the "Working Expat" may be more interested in voting for local MPs whom they can lobby and hold accountable—much more so than voting for an expat MP.

The "Long-term Expat", on the other hand, may not be as engaged or connected locally, having immigrated long before to more distant places. Their family's economic and social well-being is mostly derived from their foreign habitat not Lebanon. And while they may visit, it is less frequent than the "Working Expat". Still, they care for their homeland, want to positively help, and have plenty of resources to do so. But here's the dilemma: Whatever happens inside Lebanon may not carry as direct a consequence on their lives in the short term as it does their "Working Expat" counterpart. Therefore, one would expect that the "Long-term Expats" would be more interested in national issues than specific local district issues. For example, they would be more interested in the national education system and how their own kids can be engaged while living abroad than they would in the issue of a specific school in a specific district in Lebanon. They would be interested in cultural exchange with their own communities abroad having Lebanon act as a conduit providing network externalities. They would be interested in trade and employment that would help Lebanon; but more interested if it could provide their expat constituency investment, staffing, or business expansion opportunities. None of these may be priorities for local MPs. And so "Long-term Expats" are unlikely to be lured by MPs whose agendas and focus may be acutely local. Instead, they would prefer to vote for an MP from among their own. They would prefer someone they can more easily listen to, understand, lobby, and hold responsible for their interests in Lebanon as well as their expat jurisdiction.

Considering these two equally important Lebanese expat profiles and needs, wouldn't giving expats the choice to vote for their type of MP—local or expat—be the correct way of proceeding?

Some may question this logic; others may call it complex. It shouldn't be. As it stands, the embassies are providing their expats with the possibility of voting for any of the local Lebanese districts to which they officially registered (as per the law of 2008). Giving them a choice simply means adding one more district (their expat jurisdiction). Upon registering, the expat simply chooses which district they would like to vote in (local or expat). And come vote time, the lists are provided with that voters name in the proper list with the said voter voting in the corresponding ballot box. It adds very little administrative burden to the foreign missions. Indeed, those calling for tripling the districts in Lebanon would arguably create a much bigger burden on Lebanon's diplomatic missions than giving choice to the expats.

This said, on average what will more likely occur is that "Working Expats" clustered in the Gulf and parts of Eastern Europe and Africa would tend to prefer to vote for the local districts inside of Lebanon, which they and their families are still very closely associated with. Whereas those in the Americas, Western Europe, and Australia will tend to choose the expat district(s), because they may have lost touch with any of the local districts. This logically implies that the sum total ballot boxes will likely be less than what the current 2008 law suggests of all foreign missions allowing registration for all local districts.

The question of course is what would happen if the government insists on all expats voting only for local districts (based on the current 2008 law), which has all the expats in one bucket voting for the current 128 local MP slots. If that proves to be the case, in all likelihood, the law will fail to attract many expats to register or vote, as indeed actually occurred with registration rates at embassies anemically less than 0.05% of the potential. But here it is very important to understand that this is not because expats do not care about their homeland (especially the Type II Long-term Expats), but because many will continue to feel disenfranchised. And since the Type II expats live in societies where votes matter and where they have representatives that understand and work towards attaining their needs, they are not going to accept regressing into casting votes for the same old Lebanese system, which in so many ways was one of the root causes behind them leaving their homeland to begin with.

The Lebanese President and the cabinet have done well and need to be commended on introducing a progressive election bill almost a year before the upcoming parliamentary elections. Its expat component which calls for electing six new expat MPs is a brave new step and has the potential for introducing innovative and well-needed change in a country that desperately needs it. For it to work, however, it is crucial the following be confirmed:

1) Expats will be given their own district(s).

2) Expats will be given Representatives for these districts.

3) Expats will be given the choice to either register to vote for an MP from their expat district or for a local Lebanese district.

How to Revive Expat Interest in Lebanon (December 2012)

In recently made public statements, Lebanese officials have been questioning whether the Lebanese Expat community is interested in participating in Lebanon's future. After all, only 10,000 out of a potential hundreds of thousands—not to say millions—actually registered to vote as expats. Perhaps the real question these officials need to be asking is this one: What do we need to do in order to attract and engage the Lebanese expat community, which continues to sustain Lebanon's economy providing it with almost a quarter of its annual GDP, hundreds of thousands of annual visitors, billions of dollars of banking deposits, and ample international support during war crises?

The answer to the above questions depends on three basic things that expats are demanding from their homeland: Appreciation, Participation, and Representation.

Appreciation: When it comes to appreciation, most Lebanese expats feel their homeland has never appreciated them enough. In fact, the pervasive feeling in our community is that the homeland sees us as a resource only worthy of milking. Until the day the country realizes that expat help is a choice expats make and not an obligation they owe, the premise of the relationship between expats and the homeland will always remain precarious and will only weaken with time.

Participation: The absence of respect and appreciation has resulted in a lack of participation. For the longest time and while providing so much, Lebanese expats were not even given the vote. In the United States, named the land of opportunity, work and residency visas (quickly followed by citizenship) have been allowed for the mere investment of $100,000. In our homeland, $8 billion of our annual expat remittances have not been enough to merit expats the vote. Even worse, our expat sisters and daughters, who are married to foreigners, are not even allowed to give their children the Lebanese citizenship. At a time when our adoptive nations from North to South America, Europe, Africa, and all the way to Australia have given us all kinds of rights not least of which is the right to vote inside and outside their borders, our Lebanese homeland recognizing that right in 2008 has seen governments—current and previous—drag their feet in its deployment as if the nation were being led to a guillotine. The tragedy of the matter is that most people in Lebanon recognize that the expats may be the only thing that would actually drag them away from the political, economic, and social guillotine hanging over the nation. And if that were not enough, the expats are bound by the registration restrictions and deadlines, at a time when the government has not even defined what, how, and who expats should be voting for and under what law. The message from many expats to Lebanon is this: With such disrespect, many prefer not to participate at all.

Representation: So far, under the 2008 law, the plan is to have expats vote for the same 128 MPs in each of their ancestral Lebanese districts. While there is a September 2012 cabinet bill pending ratification, which would indeed give the Lebanese expats their own representatives, some believe it will not pass. So here's the question: Even if expats are given the right to vote, of what consequence would the vote be to them? In other words, what benefit would Lebanese expats get voting for a member of parliament who serves a geographic constituency they do not live in, do not participate in, and have no implications from whatsoever? Some will argue it is principal. Unfortunately, that's not enough. Expats will vote if there is a fundamental interest that directly benefits them. Otherwise there's no point and they don't have time to waste. The French, Italian even the Tunisian diasporas (all of which are proportionately much less influential to their homelands than the Lebanese expats) have all accepted expat representatives to engage their expat communities. Canada and Ireland are all seriously considering it. Why? Out of the interest and necessity that globalization brings and their need to engage economically, socially, and politically.

Borders are quickly fading and populations becoming more and more fluid. Having representatives in different global regions allows for stronger links and deeper engagement. Lebanese expats need representatives that understand their unique needs and can help them help the homeland. And Lebanon needs expat MPs who are serving these constituencies. To expect an MP in Akkar, or Bab el Tibbeneh, or Saida, or Hermel, or any other specific voting Lebanese district to understand the needs of the Lebanese constituencies in Brazil, Australia, and North America is foolhardy. And if that were the hope, why has it never happened so far in Lebanon's history? Bottom line, the Lebanese expats reject representation through local MPs who have no idea of their needs, mindset, potential, or ambitions for the homeland; and they refuse to be boxed into the divisive sectarianism that our indigenous brethren have been forced to accept locally.

In conclusion, the message to Lebanon and its government is this: While the emotional link to our homeland is there, in this globalized world, it is increasingly tenuous. Milking the expat resources dry based on a fading emotional attachment without commensurate appreciation, participation, and representation is becoming old. If Lebanon wants to tap the expats' economic power through network externalities, show them the respect they deserve, and which the entire world has recognized through their hard-earned work.

You want their voice to be heard, give them the vote. And you want their sustained participation, give them their representatives.

ACKNOWLEDGEMENTS

Acknowledgements

I dedicated this book to two people whom I love dearly. Many years ago, when I left Lebanon to come to the United States with my sister, it was my aunt Zaynab and uncle Rabi Shatila who welcomed us into their home, took care of us, and taught us the ways of an orderly world. I am sure it was not easy for them to remold into civil society two highly strung teenagers coming from a war-torn nation, ones who had barely experienced the normalcy of modern life—not even driving through traffic lights! They succeeded nonetheless; and I am forever indebted to the both of them for not getting a traffic ticket in years! This debt grows unabated as I continue to seek their counsel on so many matters—not least of which are all the engaging conversations, which are an inspiration to my writing.

I would also like to thank Rami Khoury, current editor at large of the Daily Star in Lebanon and Director of the Issam Fares School of Public Policy at the American University of Beirut. Rami and I met many years ago at Harvard's Kennedy School of Government where he was doing a fellowship; and I was finishing my graduate studies. I shared with him some of my writings, which he was kind enough to edit and publish on numerous occasions in the Daily Star. In so doing, he encouraged me to continue writing and share my ideas—even when some of them were quite unorthodox. For this, he has my admiration and gratitude. Michael Young would eventually take over the Op-Ed section at the Daily Star and around the time of the Cedar Revolution continued to publish several of my pieces, which I also appreciate.

A thank-you also goes out to Raja Kamal, at the time at Harvard's Kennedy School of Government for all his time, and the Hariri Foundation in the USA, especially Rafic Bizri and David Thompson, who in the year

2000 believed in a young scholar's grandiose plans to lead a Harvard team to analyze Lebanon's maladies. They were generous enough to underwrite the summer practicum and open doors to many an interview with Lebanese policy makers. It was an experience I will never forget.

I would also like to thank Theresia Riesenhuber for editing the very first manuscript of this book; as well as Thomas Peters at the Morisken Verlag for his valuable guidance during the publishing process.

While I recognize and appreciate much input from all of those mentioned and from so many more over the past decade, I take full responsibility for all the opinions herein represented.

And last but certainly not least, I would like to extend a very warm thank you to all my readers. Whether they agree or disagree with what I write, the mere fact they are open enough to read another's opinion are signs of intellectual curiosity and receptivity, both of which I highly value and believe to be keystones of any civilized society.